Mind in Action

Mind in Action

JEFF COULTER

HUMANITIES PRESS INTERNATIONAL, INC.
Atlantic Highlands, NJ

Copyright © Jeff Coulter, 1989

First published 1989 in the United States of America
by Humanities Press International Inc.,
Atlantic Highlands, NJ 07716

Library of Congress Cataloging in Publication Data

Coulter, Jeff
  Mind in action.
    1. Cognition – Social aspects. 2. Knowledge, Sociology
  of. I. Title.
  BF311.C697 1989   302   89–11106
  ISBN 0–391–03656–4
  ISBN 0–391–03657–2 (pbk.)

Printed in Great Britain

Contents

Preface

This book is intended for advanced students of the behavioral sciences – sociology, social and cognitive psychology, social anthropology – and philosophy. It is not, however, a textbook, nor a neutral presentation of a collection of themes and arguments. Rather, it is to be read as an argumentative introduction, from a sociological point of view, to a variety of currently debated topics in the study of cognitive phenomena.

I have several acknowledgements to make before we get down to business. I should like to express my thanks to Dr David Held and the editors of Polity Press for giving me this opportunity to present these ideas in the form in which they appear. I owe a debt to the University of Lancaster for their gracious hospitality over two summers during which I had occasion to argue about these topics with resident faculty in philosophy and the social sciences as an Honorary Senior Research Fellow. I am especially grateful to Dr John Hughes and Professor John Urry for their kindness in providing me with an amicable environment in which to work. I am also grateful to my own institution, Boston University, for my appointment to a Humanities Foundation Senior Fellowship (1987–88), which facilitated my work while serving as Chair of my Department, a task which, as any chairperson will attest, is not normally conducive to scholarly productivity. My thanks, as well, to a remarkable cohort of graduate students at Boston University who kept me honest during my 'Wittgenstein and Social Science' seminar series (1987), and whose many contributions have undoubtedly honed my thinking about these matters.
Some fragments of the following chapters have been presented as

lectures. The section on information processing and the remarks on research on hypnosis formed the basis of a presentation to the Eighth International Institute for Ethnomethodology at Andover, Mass., August 1987. The discussion of 'personality' formed the basis of a lecture presented to the Department of Sociology, Boston University, November 1987, and some fragments of other chapters were woven together and delivered as a lecture on Ethnomethodology and Social Construction to the Center for European Studies, Harvard University, December, 1987.

I wish to thank Professors Stephen Turner and Michael Lynch for their most helpful comments on various aspects of this work. As always, I owe more than an intellectual debt to my wife, Dr Lena Jayyusi. Naturally, no one shares any responsibility whatever for the contents of this book.

Jeff Coulter
Boston, Mass.

Introduction

This book is designed to be an introduction to a range of arguments and analytical topics in the contemporary sociology of knowledge and, in particular, to some current themes arising out of a radical reworking of classical precepts about the nature and role of the individual subject and his[1] cognitive, mental and experiential attributes. In trespassing extensively onto psychological territory, we shall follow Goffman's recommendation and avoid that 'touching tendency to keep a part of the world safe from sociology'[2] – in this case, the 'mind' of man.

In pursuing our inquiries, we shall present arguments many of which may appear primarily philosophical in character. In large measure, contemporary issues in the sociology of knowledge (as it has developed since Schutz, and Berger and Luckmann) are quite abstract and take on the significance they have primarily in relation to themes arising out of epistemology (the theory of knowledge), the philosophy of science, philosophy of action and philosophy of mind. In the present treatment, focusing as it does extensively on the possibility of a radical sociology of the 'cognizing subject', contributions (both useful and problematic) of influential work in the philosophy of mind must be examined. To a considerable extent, then, the discussions to be presented here are inter- or cross-disciplinary in character. Proposals from conceptual grammar, psychology and cognitive science, phenomenology, ethnomethodology and related fields will be outlined and assessed in terms of the project of establishing a specifically *sociological* understanding of the human subject and his mental endowments.

It is perhaps worthwhile at the outset to state what is not going to

be attempted here. First, no systematic overview of ethnomethodology will be provided. There are now at least three reliable texts
which make such an overview superfluous here.[3] In so far as
ethnomethodological concepts and concerns are invoked in the
present work, I have tried to make them as self-contained and as
contextually clear as possible. Readers seeking fuller expositions of
this complex field are urged to consult these excellent texts.
Secondly, I have avoided any detailed examination of those areas
within Critical Social Theory that are occasionally concerned with
cognate topics. In particular, I have precluded the work of
Habermas and the Frankfurt School; the secondary literature here
is already enormous, and it would have been too great a digression
to seek to do justice to it here, especially since, in my view at least,
we need to take a relatively uncluttered second look at several
fundamental issues in the theoretical treatment of mind, cognition
and social action. Thirdly, although I shall have little to say about
the contributions of Michel Foucault, I fully endorse and sympa-
thize with Hacking's characterization of Foucault's project:

He wants to know how the subjects themselves are constituted. Just as
there was no pure madness, no thing-in-itself, so there is no pure subject,
no 'I' or 'me' prior to the forms of description and action appropriate to a
person. Literary historians have long noted that a person did not conceive
of himself as a poet – as *that* kind of person – before the Romantic era.
One just wrote poems. Liberationists urge that the category of 'homosexual' (and hence 'heterosexual') did not exist until the doctors of deviancy
invented it. There were acts, but not a homosexual *kind* of person. It is a
Foucaultian thesis that every way in which I can think of myself as a person
and an agent is something that has been constituted within a web of
historical events. Here is one more step in the destruction of Kant: the
noumenal self is nothing.[4]

One theme to be developed in this book is the presentation of a case
for this kind of thinking, but shorn of much of the conventional
structuralist imagery. There is, however, a further step to be taken,
which is to show that the identification and individuation of the
mental cannot be independent of the social, cultural and historical
environments of persons, and then to take stock of the sociological
significance of that proposal.

Let me, then, outline the structure of this text.

Chapter 1 introduces the general intellectual context for most of
what follows. Here, I seek to specify some of the major shifts

involved in the transition from classical preoccupations in the sociology of knowledge to the modern extension of its domain to encompass the cognitive properties of a huge variety of human social practices, and the transformation of its focal interest from, e.g., specifically political ideologies and doctrines to *any* significant recurring conceptual or epistemic creation of human agents in social relationships. This transformation is elaborated in chapter 2, where a further, primarily methodological, shift is noted and argued for: a shift away from causal-explanatory strategies and toward a greater interest in the *logic* of the achievement of 'intelligibility' in social life. This is exemplified in two ways. First, Bloor's program for a causal sociology of (scientific) knowledge is subjected to critical scrutiny, and, second, aspects of the logic of the organization of socially distributed knowledge and belief are discussed, arising out of the classical problem of imputation and the problem of the sociality and historicity of knowledge-claims. If, as we now would claim, intelligibility is essentially *inter*subjective, and cognition is, in neglected dimensions, fundamentally 'practical' and tied to organizations of social activities in analysable ways, then a proper investigative strategy into the achievement of intelligibility in the social world would involve the specification of 'grammars' of practical cognition. This idea is elaborated, and what is argued to be a misleading form of the dichotomy of a prioristic versus empirical inquiry in this domain is undermined. The domain of inquiry appropriate for an epistemic sociology is proposed to consist in the *logic* of living together and socially constituting the intelligibility of the world in any of its aspects.

The stage is now (I hope) set for a radical reconstruction of our conception of the nature and role of the human subject in society. In chapter 3, I confront several influential themes in the conceptualization of the human subject, within symbolic interaction theory (especially Blumer's originating conceptions), neo-Cartesian philosophy of mind, and computational cognitive science of the kind drawing its inspiration from Turing, Shannon and developments in Artificial Intelligence. Recurring misconceptions about the interpretive character of human (social) action, the nature of meaning and understanding, the putative privacy of our language of experience, the nature of rule-following, and the so-called unconscious processing of information in humans, are systematically unravelled. A common theme – that of the 'sovereignty of the individual subject' – is identified and challenged. This challenge is further developed in chapter 4, where the concept of 'criterial satisfaction' is introduced and put to work. This is related to the vexed question of first-person characterizations of the mental. Key resources here have been the writings of Cavell and Hacker. Subsequently, the idea that our socioculturally standardized ways of using our mental and experiential conceptual apparatus embody a 'folk psychology', a kind of implicit ontology, theory or metaphysics of mind, is subjected to critical scrutiny. It is argued that grammars of concept formation and deployment in this domain do not *embody* or entail any 'theories', defective or correct, although they remain historical, human constructions.

In chapter 5, the concepts of 'personality' are examined in terms of their use in mundane, social intercourse and in theoretical schemes in the human sciences. Here, the primacy of 'praxis' (practical activities)[5] over the supposedly 'sovereign' individual comes to the fore. It is claimed that invocations of personality operate in analysable ways in practical discourse, but that, within widely-used *theoretical* discourses, it cannot be seen to function as a genuinely explanatory concept without distortion. The abiding notion of a personality as a core, essence or noumenon is discarded in favor of a praxiological, constructionist account.

A similar effort at de-reification is undertaken in chapter 6, in which we return to a more systematic consideration of the problem of the properties of mind as in some sense 'real' phenomena. The derivative dichotomy of realism versus social construction is opposed, and mind/brain identity theorizing (especially the recent claims advanced by Searle) and research into 'hypnotic trance' (notably Spanos and Wagstaff) are taken as cases of interest.

In the final chapter of the book, I am concerned with a cluster of issues pertaining to the idea that human actions can be given causal explanations, and that 'agents' real reasons' for actions form a species of causal account. An implicitly mentalistic form of objectivism about 'having reasons for action' is discerned in Davidson's classic version of this claim. After taking up and opposing this (Davidsonian) position, I argue that a classical line within sociology has involved assuming that agents' reasons for their actions must be subjected to a methodological rule of skepticism and *bypassed* in favor of one or another form of 'sociological' causality. (We saw this kind of reasoning at work in chapter 2 in Bloor's arguments about the proper form of a sociology of knowledge.) However, as soon as such a move is made, it confronts us with a conundrum: we have merely *stipulated* the generic unacceptability of agents' reasons as 'correct explanations' of their actions, and then we face the problem of reconciling (or in some other way expressing the nature of the relationship between) our external, causal accounts of agents' activities and their own, 'in-house' reasons for them wherever the latter may vernacularly be acceptable or accepted. If we take seriously the observation that agents' reasons *can* be correct accounts of their activities, it appears as though our problem then becomes one of detecting where and when they *are* correct according to some generally usable procedure. In the absence of such a generically usable procedure, we appear to be driven to saying such obviously indefensible things as: 'agents' reasons are correct when enough other agents grant their correctness' (as if majority rule *makes* something true), or simply stipulating (again) a unilateral attribution of 'correctness' (or 'incorrectness') using our own uncodifiable, contextually variable standards of judgement. Rather than falling into either trap, it is proposed instead that serious attention be given to the observation that agents' reason-giving practices are *themselves* kinds of social actions along with the actions for which reasons may be given. Instead of seeking to adjudicate the rightness or wrongness of agents' reasons for some decontextualized purposes, we should attend instead to the elucidation of 'reason-giving' as comprising varieties of rule-governed practices in which we participate. In focusing upon 'reason-giving-and-receiving' as kinds of social praxis in their own right, we can delineate the ways in which, for agents themselves (or, better, for agents *ourselves*) operating with a particular language and cultural resources, the manifold distinctions between a 'real' and an 'apparent' reason, between a good reason and a mere rationalization, between an acceptable reason and a poor reason, are effected within social circumstances of identifiable sorts and comprise practical devices of reasoning and judgement whose validity is variously decided where decisions of *that* kind are intelligible and appropriate. Once more, we find that sociological explanation becomes, or merges into, or is even to be replaced by, socio-logical explication. In undertaking such explication, it is quickly seen that a mentalistic metaphysics of psychological phenomena, supposedly comprising agents' 'real reasons' for their actions, evaporates.

The approach to mind, the mental, the subjective and the individual being proposed and defended here is radically sociological in the sense that it places *practices* – actions, activities, interactions – rather than *persons* at the centre of its analytical attention, treating personal attributes (of mind, of character, of experience, etc.) as instantiations of, or derivative properties from, acculturated, public conduct comprising the matrix of social affairs.

This perspective is not new, and I claim no special originality for its depiction in these essays, apart from a heightened sensitivity to its sociological significance in various respects. Indeed, elements of this kind of thinking in social science date back at least to C. Wright Mills' classic essay, 'Situated Actions and Vocabularies of Motive',[6] in which he argued: 'As over against the influential conception of motives as subjective "springs" of action, motives may be considered as typical vocabularies having ascertainable functions in delimited societal situations. Human actors do vocalise and impute motives to themselves and others . . . . Rather than fixed elements "in" an individual, motives are the terms with which interpretation of conduct *by social actors* proceeds. This imputation and avowal of motives by actors are social phenomena to be explained.'[7] In contemporary idioms, this passage has a strikingly ethnomethodological and neo-Wittgensteinian resonance. As a critical insight into the sociological possibilities for handling problems of subjectivity, the mental, the cognitive, it simply remained to be extended, with appropriate modifications and corrections, to encompass the full range of the mental attributes, properties and dispositions of persons analysed traditionally in wholly psychologistic terms *even within sociology*. A key issue in the battle over 'psychologism' in this connection has been the propensity of psychologistic theorizing to treat persons as 'possessors' of such attributes and properties in an unproblematic manner, abstracted from the sociohistorical, sociocultural and interactional-communicative circumstances within which *alone* they become, for laypersons and professionals alike, visible, ascribable, rationally avowable, ratifiable, defeasible, inferrable – in other words, 'available'.[8] This development of a fully *sociological* understanding of the mental, subjective and cognitive aspects of persons, foreshadowed in the thought of Mead, Mills and other, largely unselfconsciously non-Cartesian scholars, presages a redrawing of the intellectual boundaries of the human sciences. It is this promise and prospect which animates the present intellectual project, and, along with it, the thorough demystification of so many popular but deeply mythological conceptions of human cognition.

I have, in these chapters, sought to keep the expositions and arguments relatively succinct and minimally technical. I have also tried to do justice to some of the major authors and themes, but many have, perforce, been neglected or only briefly mentioned. As such, these chapters are most profitably to be studied in relation to some of the major texts with which they deal, but in so far as possible I have striven to achieve some degree of self-containment. There are many arguments and examples which could be taken further, and none of them is uncontroversial. If they encourage further study and reflection, counter-argument or the development of more novel approaches, then these chapters will have served their intended purpose.

Notes

1 In this text, I shall follow Dorothy Smith's suggestion and employ as a generic pronomial term the one which reflects the gender of the author, thus, 'he/his/him' will be used throughout in cases where 'abstract persons' are being referred to. I shall also have recourse to 'man' as a generic term.

2 Erving Goffman, *Encounters* (Bobbs-Merrill, N.Y., 1961), p. 152.

3 John Heritage, *Garfinkel and Ethnomethodology* (Polity Press, Cambridge, England, 1984): D. Benson and J.A. Hughes, *The Perspective of Ethnomethodology* (Longman, London, 1983) and Wes Sharrock and Bob Anderson, *The Ethnomethodologists* (Key Sociologists Series: Tavistock, London, 1986).

4 Ian Hacking, 'The Archaeology of Foucault'. In David Couzens Hoy (ed.), *Foucault: A Critical Reader* (Basil Blackwell, Oxford, 1986). This is an interesting introductory collection of papers. They variously demonstrate that, in so far as there could be a 'Foucaultian' perspective in general terms, at least it shares with much ethnomethodology and 'social constructionist' thought a radical anti-psychologism.

5 In the sense of von Cieszkowski (in his *Prolegomenon zur Historiosophie*) and not Kotarbinski (in his *Praxiology* (Trans. O. Wojtasiewicz, Pergamon Press, N.Y., 1965)). See David McLellan, *The Young Hegelians and Karl Marx* (Macmillan, London, 1969), pp. 9–11, for documentation of the claim that this term, in its most common contemporary usage, was coined by von Cieszkowski.

6　C. Wright Mills, 'Situated Actions and Vocabularies of Motive'. Reprinted from *American Sociological Review*, Vol. 5, December 1940, in J.G. Manis and B.N. Meltzer (eds), *Symbolic Interaction* (Allyn & Bacon, Boston, 1967).

7　Mills, in Manis and Meltzer (eds), *Symbolic Interaction*, pp. 355–6, emphasis in original. Subsequent sociologically-oriented treatments of 'motive' in terms of socially organized (i.e. socially conventionalized and interactionally occasioned) *practices* of ascription and avowal, such as Alan Blum and Peter McHugh's well-known paper, 'The Social Ascription of Motives', *American Sociological Review*, Vol. 36, 1971, found additional sustenance from the Wittgensteinian tradition in the philosophy of mind. For a fuller characterization of this contribution to the 'sociologizing' (or 'de-psychologizing') of 'motives', see especially R.S. Peters, *The Concept of Motivation* (Routledge & Kegan Paul, London, 1958) and A.R. Louch, 'Motive'. In his *Explanation and Human Action* (Basil Blackwell, Oxford, 1966), pp. 95–104. More grist to the sociolinguistic mill was furnished, indirectly, by Kenneth Burke's pioneering literary treatment, *The Grammar of Motives* (Prentice-Hall, N.J., 1945).

8　This constitutes an extension of the ethnomethodological treatment of human actions to the domain of the mental, subjective and other 'personal' properties of human agents. For defense of the claim that it comprises a productive synthesis of ethnomethodological and Wittgensteinian insights, see my *The Social Construction of Mind* (Macmillan, London, 1979; paperback edition, 1987).

1

Epistemic Sociology

Classical precepts in the sociology of knowledge[1] have been significantly transformed in recent years, and it is worth taking stock of some of the intellectual challenges and subsequent theoretical developments which inform much current thinking in the field.

The traditional focus of the sociology of knowledge in the Mannheimian framework (at least since Mannheim's classic text, *Ideology and Utopia* (1929; first English translation by Wirth and Shils, 1936)) has been the analysis of more or less coherent, socially distributed world-views expressed in political doctrines and belief clusters in terms of their (historical) relationship to social collectivities and their interests, whether material or otherwise. Parallel themes have included the study of broader forms of consciousness (e.g. the so-called 'bureaucratic mentality', 'conservatism', 'communist ideology', the 'spirit of capitalism', the 'business ethic', etc.) along similar lines. Much of this work has been implicitly or explicitly debunking in tone, often contributing to what Habermas and others were later to call 'ideology-critique'. A less prominent aspect of the disciplinary sociology of knowledge (although significant for understanding anthropology's interest in epistemic phenomena) derives in large measure from Durkheim's *The Elementary Forms of the Religious Life: The Totemic System in Australia* (1912; first English translation by Swain, 1915). Here, the focus is at once more general and more foundational: the analysis of systems of classification as instruments of reason and their social origins.

Although many strands of argument and counter-argument, innovation and rethinking, are distributed across a variety of disciplinary pursuits under a range of diverse characterizations, it could be proposed that a novel and coherent form of inquiry into the social structuring and transmission of knowledge is emerging. We may refer to this as the development of a sociology of cognition[2] or, more broadly, as the rise of an epistemic sociology.

In contemporary psychological theory and research, in which the concept of 'cognition' has become a familiar term of art, cognition has been treated as an overarching rubric. In current usage, it encompasses a variety of phenomena whose conceptualizations may have only logical connections with the concept of 'knowledge', such as: comprehension, memory, perception, intelligence and reasoning. This, it seems to me, is a very sensible expansion of interest beyond that of classical sociology's primary foci. However, it is fair to note that the traditional sociology of knowledge was, almost from its inception, a gloss for an interest in 'belief(s)', 'doctrines', 'ideologies' (and 'utopias'), 'theories', 'theodicies', and related topics not properly subsumable under a strictly rendered concept of 'knowledge' alone, whether we speak of the Mannheimian, Durkheimian, Mertonian or related programs of inquiry. Toulmin argues that an intellectual interest in what he terms 'epistemics' has:

necessarily [been] an area of interdisciplinary enquiry. Half a dozen disciplines have epistemic aspects, sectors or implications – e.g., the physiology of perception, the sociology of knowledge, and the psychology of concept formation. Like cosmology and matter-theory, epistemics is also a very long-lived subject. For twenty-five centuries, the problem of human understanding has been an enduring preoccupation: a permanent feature of men's speculative thought, ramifying in many directions, but preserving a recognizable unity and continuity.[3]

Current foci in the epistemic 'sector' of sociology include the development of the Sociology of Science[4], the Sociology of Communications Media[5] (a field which has only very recently become influenced by modern tenets in the sociology of knowledge, and which I shall therefore preclude from extensive discussion), Ethnomethodological studies of practical communicative conduct and practical reasoning in social settings[6] and the closely-related domain of 'social constructionist' thinking in sociology and social psychology.[7] In social and cultural anthropology, cognitive anthropology and ethnoscience have been heralded as significant intellectual epistemic developments within the conduct of ethnography (the naturalistic description of the culture of a people or of an institution or group within a society). Anthropology's long-standing analytical interest in the nature of culture is transformed thereby into a concern for the organization of cultural knowledge as manifested in specific conventions or patterns of linguistic usage in relation to a variety of objects, situations and practices. Ethnoscience, especially, treated 'folk' knowledge of a variety of types as pre-theoretical conceptual schemata whose rules of use were to be rendered explicit by the analyst. This became a significant point of connection with investigations of cognitive phenomena elsewhere in the human sciences, and it developed rapidly within the otherwise predominantly social-structuralist, functionalist and evolutionist frameworks of anthropological thought and research[8]. And, within psychology, cognitive science probably holds the field as the most important and expanding component of that discipline[9]. We shall discuss this development in some detail later.

My intention in what follows is to chart several theoretical innovations which, taken together, set the stage for the emergence of novel forms of empirical, epistemic inquiry, aspects of which will be described subsequently.

The Discovery of Everyday Knowledge as Sociological Phenomenon

Several themes which arose out of theoretical debate within and about the sociology of knowledge during the decade of the greatest intellectual foment within the recent history of the social sciences, the 1960s, need to be addressed. I circumscribe my topics in this way, and according to this particular time-frame, because what I would argue to be the single most influential and effective theoretical breakthrough in the field originated then. This was the abandonment of the policy of studying only *specialized* bodies of knowledge and belief of a political, ethical and/or philosophical character to the exclusion of all other epistemic or cognitive phenomena, and the emergence of a serious analytical interest in *any* form of socially distributed and socially transmitted conceptualisations.

In their path-breaking critical treatment of the problematics of the traditional sociology of knowledge, Berger and Luckmann observe that: 'Only a very limited group of people in any society engages in theorizing, in the business of "ideas", and the construction of *Weltanschauungen*. But everyone in society participates in its "knowledge" in one way or another.'[10]

In elaborating this focus upon the everyday 'life-world' and its constitution by commonsense reason, Berger and Luckmann, drawing upon some of the ideas of the philosopher-sociologist Alfred Schutz, state that: '[C]ommonsense "knowledge" rather than "ideas" must be the central focus for the sociology of knowledge. It is precisely this 'knowledge' that constitutes the fabric of meanings without which no society could exist.'[11] Despite the unnecessary restriction which Berger and Luckmann here seem to place upon the notion of 'ideas', appearing to restrict 'ideas' to the category of abstract intellectual or theoretical productions alone, the general point is clear: in Harold Garfinkel's terms, we are to 'place the sociology of knowledge at the heart of the sociological enterprise with full seriousness'.[12] Alfred Schutz, whose work on the epistemological foundations of sociology served as the inspiration for this reconstrual of the proper topic of an empirical sociology of knowledge,[13] had proposed that *everything* comprising a society member's social (and natural) environment is known to him through the medium of 'typifications' or 'common-sense constructs of typicality'.[14] Language, as the primary social medium for the formation, acquisition, articulation, communication and transformation of concepts, now takes its place as a foundational phenomenon within any sociology of knowledge and of human cognitive conduct more generally, and so a sociologist's primary task is the elucidation of 'Intersubjectivity, interaction, intercommunication, and language [which] are simply presupposed as the unclarified foundation of [existing sociological] theories.'[15]

Since it is the ideas, typifications or concepts which people have that enable them to interact, speak, reason and otherwise conduct themselves together to comprise social arrangements, relationships and settings in orderly ways, *including being able to observe them and make sense of them in the first instance*, the sociology of 'commonsense' knowledge is intimately connected to the investigation of actual, socially organized conduct. But how are such inquiries to proceed? What are the forms of these postulated connections between 'concepts', 'commonsense knowledge' and practical social activities and interactions?

Various answers to these questions were forthcoming, but few retained the classical causal, quasi-causal or motivational conceptions in which knowledge/belief and actual conduct were related theoretically.[16] Instead, commonsense knowledge expressible in commonsense concepts is seen neither in primarily motivational nor causal terms, but as *constitutive* of the very possibility of meaningful conduct and of a meaningful environment. By stressing the nature of this primary relationship, Schutz, and those who followed his leads on this issue, was able to exhibit clearly the connection between meaning (as intelligibility) and socially shared conceptualization: the old Weberian problematic of *verstehen* (how is the sociologist to ascertain the meaning of an action, social object or situation to the agent(s) operating to produce them?) now becomes an empirical research topic: how do agents themselves ascertain the meaning(s) of their own and each others' conduct, objects and situations in the varieties of orderly, conventional ways in which they actually do this? The achievement of intersubjective comprehension – which itself is the achievement of some form of *knowledge* – however locally transient or globally significant – is seen as facilitated by social participation in conventional *grammars of conceptualization*.

Schutz, and Berger and Luckmann after him, did not elaborate a research strategy in any detail, and restricted themselves to discussing propositional or, in Schutz's terms, 'recipe' knowledge of various kinds. For example, Schutz proposes that:

All our knowledge of the world, in common-sense as scientific thinking, involves constructs, i.e., a set of abstractions, generalizations, formalizations, idealisations specific to the respective level of thought organisation. Strictly speaking, there are no such things as facts, pure and simple. All facts are from the outset facts selected from a universal context by the activities of our mind. They are, therefore, always interpreted facts, either facts looked at as detached from their context by an artificial abstraction or facts considered in their particular setting. . . . This does not mean that, in daily life or in science, we are unable to grasp the reality of the world. It just means that we grasp merely certain aspects of it, namely those which are relevant to us either for carrying on our business of living or from the point of view of a body of accepted rules of procedure of thinking called the method of science.[17]

In this and similar passages in his writings about knowledge, society and culture, Schutz sustains the traditional focus upon conceptual, propositional, discursively available, 'factual' and prosaic 'knowledge(s)'.

However, when considering the forms of relationship between modalities of knowledge and practical activities, such a restriction to the propositional or discursive modes became limiting. We shall take up this issue further on. Suffice to say at this point that not everything we call 'knowledge' is conceptual knowledge: knowing *how* to do things can be distinguished from knowing *that* X is the case, and, in everyday, practical affairs the former kind of knowledge is at least as important to understand and to analyse as the latter. For the moment, however, let us concentrate upon one essential aspect of the 'post-Schutz' sociology of knowledge: its stress upon language and communication generally as media of social conceptualization and 'commonsense knowledge' in human affairs.

In a famous monograph, Peter Winch offered the following observation:

I have linked the assertion that social relations are internal [conceptual] with the assertion that men's mutual interaction 'embodies ideas', suggesting that social interaction can more profitably be compared to the exchange of ideas in a conversation than to the interaction of forces in a physical system. This may seem to put me in danger of over-intellectualising social life, especially since the examples I have so far discussed have all been examples of behavior which expresses *discursive* ideas, that is, ideas which also have a straightforward linguistic expression. It is because the use of language is so intimately, so inseparably, bound up with the other, non-linguistic activities which men perform, that *it is possible to speak of their non-linguistic behavior also as expressing discursive ideas.*[18]

This general insight is clearly coeval with the Schutzian position on the centrality of commonsense knowledge and typifications (concepts) mentioned earlier, but opens up the possibility of a sociology of action, interaction and communication in which the rule-governed concepts of human social action, amongst many other operably relevant concepts, figure as constitutive of non-discursive as well as discursive conduct for its producers and witnesses in any social setting whatsoever. This point requires elaboration.

The rules which make an action what it *is* are not reducible to any (set of) descriptions of physiological or physical transformations, since virtually any 'action' or 'activity' can be realized through *different* transformations (the exceptions being marginal cases such as 'winking' and the like), and the converse is also true (i.e. that the same physiological or physical transformations can amount to the production of different actions or activities). Consider the following organic-behavioral movements: I pick up a metal object in my right hand, enfold it, align it with my arm extended at right angles to my upright body, grasp its protrusion with the finger closest to my thumb, squeeze it and discharge a bullet at you. This exact (quasi-)physiological description of my action may remain identical under the following transformations of its nature: 'wounding you', 'murdering you', 'executing you' (aside from rhetorical claims that all executions are acts of murder), 'shooting you without any intention of killing you', 'perpetrating euthanasia', 'killing you accidentally' (during a stage-play where someone had maliciously substituted live ammunition for blank cartridges), 'engaging in target practice', 'combat', and many other possible characterizations. Similarly, by extending my arm and displaying my palm outwards towards you and moving it from right to left subtending an arc of 30 degrees, I may be: 'waving goodbye', 'greeting a friend', 'trying to attract your attention', 'giving a signal', etc. Conversely, the single, self-same activity of, say, 'greeting a friend', can be realized in and through a wide range of diverse postural, gestural, linguistic and paralinguistic productions. Thus, whilst indeed our biological equipment (or specific surrogates) are essential to our capacity to perform actions, its dispositions and transformations are never definitive of what such actions *are*. Instead, the rules which make of social actions whatever actions they are must be *the rules of use of the concepts of those actions shared by the acting agents in a language and culture*. One does not have to possess the concept of 'blinking' in order to be said to have blinked – blinking is a physical event, and not an action, even though it is something which we may be said to have *done* – but the concept of 'winking' must be shared in the culture within which the conduct so identified has occurred for it to have been rationally ascribed. To be able to see that someone is engaged in 'bartering' (and not, say, 'exchanging gifts') requires attribution to him of *the concept of* 'bartering', the possession of which is the ability to use that concept properly (e.g. in describing what one saw correctly, in being able to justify one's distinction between 'barter' and 'gift-giving' if required to do so, etc.). *Knowing what* people are doing (including oneself) is *knowing how* to identify what they are doing in the categories of a natural language, which requires *knowing how* to use those categories in discursive contexts, which includes *knowing when* to utter them. All of these types of knowledge are logically interrelated. They are all constitutive of human conduct.

This integral linkage between what an action is (or what it could possibly, conventionally *be*) for those engaged in it, and how it could be 'made sense of' for anyone producing or witnessing it (correctly, appropriately, properly, rationally, etc.), forms a central insight of Garfinkel's programme of ethnomethodology (the study of the logic of practical action and practical reasoning in social affairs). As Garfinkel articulates this insight, 'the activities whereby members [of society, of a common language and culture] produce and manage settings of organized everyday affairs are identical with members' procedures for making those settings 'account-able".[19] The 'account-ability' of conduct and social arrangements (i.e., their intelligibility, describability, recognizability, etc.) is made possible by the very concepts which in turn make possible the production of such conduct and settings. I must *satisfy the criteria* for the conventional conceptualization ('account-ability' or describability) of my conduct as X-ing if indeed I may properly be said to have X-ed in the first place. And, naturally enough, the same is true for you, he, she, we and they! We shall return to consider some of the technical aspects of ethnomethodological inquiry in sociology later on.

If ethnomethodology succeeded in generating an empirical programme of sociological inquiry which placed the (reconstructed) sociology of knowledge at the heart of sociology, it may properly be thought of as a cognitive sociology. And yet the relation between ethnomethodology and other forms of cognitive investigations cannot be thought of as simply a sociological appropriation of the subject-matter of cognitive psychology: for one thing, as we shall eventually argue, it makes possible a thoroughgoing sociological conception of the 'cognising subject' which is quite alien to most forms of psychological cognitivism.

The vigorous pursuit of these insights into the relationship between everyday, commonplace human actions and the epistemic phenomena of conceptualization and practical reasoning, between social conduct and commonsense knowledge(s), opened up a vast territory for rigorous exploration. The domain of study known as 'symbolic interactionism' (a term coined by Herbert Blumer, a student of G.H. Mead's, in the 1940s) had promised much to the student of human social behavior, but had delivered only ethnographies in which 'the actor's point of view' was respected as a slogan but rarely as a technical problem. The reconstructed sociology of knowledge, with its interest in the manifold linkages between everyday action, comprehension and perception and the categories of natural language and cultural knowledge, heralded a variety of technical solutions to many vexed questions raised by action theories of many varieties: How can one study the organization of people's experiences of their world? By studying the grammars of their concepts of (their conceptual knowledge of) experience. How can one reveal agents' understandings of their social behavior in rigorous ways? By investigating, with real-world materials (audiovisual records and their transcriptions), how the situated production/organization of that behavior *in its detail* makes it (mutually) intelligible.

Much of the work of ethnomethodology concentrated upon the logic of *mundane practices* as constituted and organized by various sorts of concepts and forms of practical knowledge. We shall discuss aspects of this work further on: suffice to note here that social practices as diverse as telling stories, calling the police, deciding upon someone's guilt or innocence in a court of law, diagnosing an illness, conducting a meeting or therapy session, teaching a class, maintaining organizational records, formulating location, insulting someone, undertaking a news interview, determining a suicide, improvizing in jazz and a host of similarly commonplace types of social activity have been subjected to ethnomethodological analysis in these terms. Yet the stage was set for the reinvigoration of the sociology of *scientific* knowledge as well, along lines wholly informed by the results, methods and prospects of the reconstructed sociology of everyday knowledge.

The New Sociology of Scientific Knowledge

A fresh look at a neglected topic of the traditional approaches to the sociological study of knowledge and belief became possible which reintroduced the analysis of *specialized* knowledge into the field, but in a wholly new way: the epistemic contents of the natural sciences, logic and mathematics became approachable as bodies of knowledge informing, and informed by, relatively discrete kinds of human practices. The exemption of the *substance* or *content* of natural sciences and mathematics from sustained sociological scrutiny among the classical practitioners of the sociology of knowledge such as Mannheim, Durkheim, Stark and Merton was, as Mulkay notes in his recent (and valuable) overview,[20] a consequence of their adoption of a view of social factors as *potentially contaminating influences* upon the acquisition, distribution and use of knowledge/belief(s). (Mulkay is careful to note, however, the extent to which Mannheim, for example, wavered on this issue.)

Since the natural sciences and mathematics in particular have yielded universally acknowledged truths of many kinds, whereas the domains of politics, esthetics, ethics and philosophy (not to mention social theory itself) have yielded contestable insights and inconclusive argumentations, the role of social factors was deemed (almost) *irrelevant* to the understanding and appreciation of the epistemic content of their intellectual productions and achievements. In what was virtually an abdication of the responsibility of their field, the early sociologists of knowledge espoused a form of analytical impotence in the face of scientific, technical and mathematical constructions as social phenomena. Partly as a result of their conception of social factors as contaminating, causal influences rather than as enabling resources and constitutive features, these early thinkers shied away from addressing the content of these most esteemed epistemic products of human reason in favor of addressing such institutional, structural factors as the allocation of rewards within scientific communities, the role of 'gate-keepers' in the scientific professions, the social prerequisites for the dissemination and acceptance of the various sciences, the political and economic structures associated with certain forms of scientific production and the historical emergence of new forms of scientific enterprise and inquiry. Hardly ever were the contents of the sciences – their theories and theorems, their intellectual achievements and claims, their propositions, their models, their laws, etc. – deemed amenable to sociological scrutiny for their *sociocultural construction as such*. It was as if, on the one hand, one encountered the objective picture or story of the structure of 'reality' from the sciences, and on the other hand, the 'social' world with its array of 'peer pressures', 'economic constraints', 'merely material interests', 'status and reputational hierarchies', 'power structures' and sundry other sources of actual and potential distortion in relation to which the sciences were continually being brought into being as epistemic phenomena. Seldom in the early sociology of the sciences had it been granted that, whilst indeed various forms of distortion, bias, partisanship and irrationality do have their bases in contingent social interactions and relationships, it is also *by means of* social interactions and relations (centrally, by means of interpersonal communication) that any and all scientific knowledge, including the most objective, universal and mathematically impeccable, is constructed in the first place.

The very concepts and methodological principles, the theoretical schemata and canons of representation, the technologies and practices of controlled experimentation and the criteria for adjudication – the very internal, epistemic, cognitive or intellectual stuff of science – were, are and must inevitably be, productions of work, sociocultural in nature and thus socioculturally constituted as such.

Such a characterization does not in the least undermine any claim to universality of scope nor of objectivity of result: it is not the province of the social scientist to adjudicate such matters unilaterally. Rather, it is to note that, even for those canons, theories and laws which have attained universal assent as discovered insights into the structure of nature for the purposes of prediction, manipulation, control or technological advancement, there is no exemption from their embeddedness within and answerability to concerted human reasoning, perception, conduct and communication as their *necessary* media for conceptual constitution, assessment, transmission and transformation. Universality, truth and objectivity are, after all, themselves socially bestowed properties and none the worse for that. To remark of some phenomenon or its properties that it has been 'socially constructed' is *not* thereby to say that it has been relegated to the status of 'mere' artifact or the 'arbitrary' upshot of social consensus. The pejorative connotation of the concept of an 'artifact' in the experimental sciences and the fallacy of the 'consensus theory of truth' in epistemology should not blind us to the fact that, in a significant sense, 'objective findings', 'absolute mathematical truths' or 'reality-determinations' are rendered possible *only* by the acculturated, concept-laden and fundamentally social (because communicative and intersubjective) operations of their producers and consumers. The interest of this for epistemically-minded social scientists lies precisely in elucidating *how* this is so. Paradoxically, it was Sir Karl Popper whose philosophy of science perhaps did most to stress the public character of the institutions of scientific rationality,[21] but whose philosophy of *social* science was profoundly anchored to methodological individualism as an antidote to the reifications, teleological implications and simple determinisms of what he termed 'historicism', 'collectivism' or 'mob psychology'. It had yet to be appreciated that sociology's conceptual armamentarium did not need to be restricted to reifying social determinisms and (often debunking) 'interest' assignations on the one hand, nor to individualizing or psychological reconstructions on the other, when considering epistemic phenomena of any kind. The notion of the social construction of reality, as an extension of the phenomenological concept of (phenomenal) 'constitution' to the sociocultural realm of the constitution of intelligibility, enriched the possibilities of analysis, as did the sociologically suggestive work of Thomas Kuhn on 'paradigms'[22] and its affinities to the Wittgensteinian themes of socially shared concepts embodied in diverse 'language-games' and of 'the autonomy of grammar' from any putatively unmediated 'determination' by 'reality'.[23] In addition, the focus upon *conceptual* constitution, rather than the (Husserlian) phenomenological focus upon 'the constitution of phenomena by consciousness', paved the way for the development of a view of social and cultural arrangements of communication as enablements of, and not just constraints upon, scientific (as well as other epistemic) creations.

Studies of the negotiation of the meanings of 'competent scientific experiments',[24] of the derivation of 'proper scientific knowledge-claims' from 'research findings',[25] of the conceptual devices employed in justifying claims to scientificity,[26] of the accounting practices of a scientific community,[27] of the situated communicative and judgemental operations involved in the determination of the facticity of a previously postulated or hypothetical phenomenon,[28] of the properties of communicative interaction and instrumental operations which co-constitute 'laboratory work' and the emergence of research findings in the first instance[29] and of the social corroboration of 'discovery' claims in science,[30] to name but a few recent topics of inquiry, all seek to make concrete (albeit in different ways) a study policy according to which, in Garfinkel's terms, '[T]he social scientist treats knowledge, and the procedures that societal members use for its assembly, test, management and transmission, as objects of theoretical sociological interest.'[31]

Tacit and Non-Propositional Knowledge as Investigable Phenomena

We mentioned earlier the distinction between knowing-that (what, etc.) and knowing-how. The inclusion of a concern for *non*-propositional or 'practical' knowledge, Ryle's famous category of 'knowing-how', was soon to be made.[32] Theoretical nutrition for this move was available elsewhere in the human sciences and philosophy rather than in the writings of these thinkers who, under the influence of phenomenological conceptions, had shifted the field to the analysis of 'commonsense' knowledge. Beyond Ryle's initial distinction between propositional and practical knowledge, we have the contribution of Michael Polanyi to our understanding of 'tacit knowledge'[33] and the later linguistic (principally syntactic) theory of Noam Chomsky in which this idea figures in his distinction between 'linguistic competence' and 'linguistic performance'.[34]

Tacit knowledge, then, is essentially that kind of knowledge which is not available to its possessor in discursive or propositional form, but which is rather akin to 'knowing *how*'. In the case of speaking a language, for example, it may be said that while most of us know *how* to speak (in) some natural language or other, we do not thereby know *what* its syntactical principles are (at least, not in any real detail) and we do not thereby know *that* it has whatever structural properties it does have. Chomsky's analysis of native linguistic 'competence' relies upon exactly this sort of initial distinction between discursive knowledge and knowing-how-to-X. Whereas linguistic performance consists in actual speech, linguistic competence is construed as the speaker's practical mastery of the principles of the language he is using, even though the latter is articulated misleadingly by Chomsky in terms of '*unconscious* knowledge of the rules of language' in which the 'rules' are propositionally 'represented' in a speaker's mind or brain.[35]

Nonetheless, the Chomskian grammarian's goal of explicit codifi-
cation of hitherto inexplicit organizing principles involved in a
significant aspect of human social conduct – speaking a language
grammatically – becomes a model for emulation elsewhere in the
'epistemic' sectors of social-scientific thought, even though
Chomsky's own codifications of linguistic rules were more sensitive
to their amenability to mathematical (especially algebraic) model-
ing (e.g. syntax and phonology) than to their broader connections
to social-communicative (pragmatic) and conceptual (semantic,
logical) functions.

Just as the construction or design of any grammatically acceptable sentence or utterance 'embodies' epistemic principles at
different levels (syntactical, logico-grammatical), so also does the
construction of any commonplace communicative activity and
interaction. The producers of any such utterances/activities do not,
as a condition for being able to (i.e. *knowing how to*) produce
them, need to know what these describable principles might be.
Searle (a student of Chomsky's), developing J.L. Austin's analysis
of speech acts,[36] attempted to show, using hypothetical examples of
usage, how such mundane communicative activities as 'promising'
could be analysed as constituted by a set of conventional
orientations and presuppositions (codified into constitutive and
regulative rules). Ethnoscience (particularly semantic componential
analysis) in social anthropology was independently developed as
the study of the rules and principles informing the construction and
deployment of taxonomies (systems of classification) of natural and
cultural objects in different natural-language communities,[37]
(although some practitioners acknowledged having been influenced
by Chomsky's goal of formalizing 'native' intuitions[38]) and
conversation analysis (a development within Ethnomethodology
pioneered by Harvey Sacks and Emmanuel Schegloff) sought to
specify sets of rules and principles whereby coordinated communicative interaction, especially the sequential organization of such
interaction, is accomplished, as well as, relevant to this concern,
how speakers achieve intersubjectively ratified comprehension and
how they deploy natural-language categories of various kinds
(temporal, locational, personal, collective, etc.) in their talk and
establish topical coherence to this end, among other aspects of the
phenomena of interpersonal communication.[39]

Notwithstanding the importance of the primordially social phenomenon of language as 'the objective repository of vast accumulations of meaning and experience . . . [by virtue of which] accumulation a social stock of knowledge is constituted, which is transmitted from generation to generation and which is available to the individual in everyday life',[40] there are many other 'representational' media produced by, and available to, members of society both in their general capacity *as* members as well as in their particularized zones of (institutionalized) competence(s). Orthographic, pictorial, diagrammatic, photographic, filmic, textual, inscriptional, mathematical, instrumentational and other forms of representational devices, with varying degrees of dependence upon and relationship to linguistic-symbolic media, are constructed, deployed and otherwise enter into the manifold of social relations. They are also 'epistemic' social phenomena. Garfinkel's celebrated work on organizational record-keeping practices,[41] Cicourel's study of police practices and 'official records',[42] Zimmerman's analysis of record-keeping in public welfare agencies,[43] Psathas's study of 'occasioned maps',[44] Smith's discussion of the nature of documentary 'reality-construction' in modern society,[45] O'Neill's characterizations of the 'literary' production of scientific work,[46] Lynch's study of 'images' in scientific research,[47] Jayyusi's exploration of the 'socio-logic' of filmic texts[48] and other investigations of the social-epistemic functions and properties of diverse representational media and devices attest to the growing contemporary interest in them.

We find, then, a growing interest in the logic of production of epistemic phenomena, overwhelmingly communicative in nature, both 'mundane' and 'technical' (with their interrelationships). It is truly a flowering field, with enormous range and promise. At the heart of all cognition, however, is the human subject. The person is the subject both of practical and theoretical interest in respect of systems of knowledge and belief. And it is in the treatment of the person him/herself made possible by contemporary sociological thinking about cognition where we can discern its most radical thrust.

Rethinking the Cognizing Subject

In the course of some brief remarks on ethnomethodology earlier in this chapter, I mentioned that current sociological interests in 'cognition' cannot be assimilated to extant psychological conceptions of this topic of study. This is in large measure due to explorations of the implications of what has come to be known (for good or ill) as the 'social constructionist' approach to epistemic phenomena in the post-Schutzian sociology of knowledge.

Although a fuller treatment of this important topic must be postponed until later chapters, it is worth mentioning some of its parameters at this point. If any phenomenon is knowable in the first instance through our concept(s) of it expressed in a natural language, this must hold also for personal, subjective, mental and experiential phenomena. Concepts of phenomena, which alone render them intelligible, visible or otherwise available to us, are expressed in the rule-ordered or grammatical use of words or phrases in communicative occasions, and this must hold true for concepts of phenomena of a (perhaps misleadingly designated) subjective and mental nature. It was Wittgenstein who first successfully articulated the incoherence of the notion of a private mental or experiential language whose signs or symbols had meanings unique and private to each person (and perhaps differing from person to person) which could be used to refer to his or her inner world of thoughts, feelings and other subjective items of 'privileged access'.[49] We shall explore this more fully further on. For now, let us just note that members of any communication community possess the mundane capacities to discern, avow, attribute and in other ways orient to each others' thoughts, understandings, beliefs, intentions, perceptions, hopes, expectations, dreams, sensations, moods, and so on, although such capacities may be mundane, pre-reflectively exercised or 'taken for granted'. It is a central feature of what I have elsewhere termed the 'Sociology of Mind' to subject these socially shared capacities to analytical elucidation as a contribution to epistemic sociology in general.

Before proceeding to elaborate upon the origins and prospects of the sociology of mind, however, it is necessary to specify first and in some detail how the transformation of the classical sociology of knowledge into what I have been calling an epistemic sociology affects the methodological and conceptual character of such inquiries as may be collected under its rubric, especially the status of members' knowledge and beliefs as social phenomena. To that task we now turn our attention.

Notes

1 I refer here to that tradition of scholarship in the social sciences which, developing from Marx's use of the concept of 'ideology', asserts an investigable relationship between the origins and distribution of essentially sociopolitical, philosophical, theological and ethical beliefs and doctrines on the one hand, and the differential 'material' (economic, class-based) 'interests' of members of society on the other hand. For some excellent discussions of the Mannheimian, Lukácsian and related traditions in the sociology of 'ideologies' and other belief systems, see Peter Hamilton, *Knowledge and Social Structure: An Introduction to the Classical Argument in the Sociology of Knowledge* (Routledge & Kegan Paul, London, 1974); Nicholas Abercrombie, *Class, Structure and Knowledge* (Oxford, Clarendon Press, 1980); Barry Barnes, *Interests and the Growth of Knowledge* (Routledge & Kegan Paul, London, 1977); J. E. Curtis and J. W. Petras (eds), *The Sociology of Knowledge* (Duckworth, London, 1970), and, especially worthy of note for its original, non-deterministic reinterpretation of Mannheim's contribution, A. P. Simonds, *Karl Mannheim's Sociology of Knowledge* (Clarendon Press, Oxford, 1978).

2 Although Aaron Cicourel's *Cognitive Sociology* (specified in, *inter alia*, his book of the same name: Penguin, London, 1973) has important implications for current work, it is only a part of the wider enterprise I am here characterizing with a rearrangement of his proprietary title. For some discussion and critique of Cicourel's position, see Bruce N. Waller, 'Mentalistic Problems in Cicourel's Cognitive Sociology', *Journal for the Theory of Social Behavior*, Vol. 12, No. 2, July 1982.

3 Stephen Toulmin, *Human Understanding, Vol. 1: The Collective Use and Evolution of Concepts* (Princeton University Press, N.J., 1972), p. 7.

4 For an excellent overview of the development and problematics of sociology of science, see Michael Mulkay, *Science and the Sociology of Knowledge* (Allen & Unwin, London, 1979). For an exemplary research study conducted under the auspices of an (ethnomethodological) empirical interest in scientific *praxis*, see Michael Lynch,

Art and Artifact in Laboratory Science (Routledge & Kegan Paul, London, 1984).

5   For access to current directions, terms of analysis and points of argumentation in this burgeoning field of inquiry, see the debate on media studies in *Sociology*: Digby C. Anderson and W.W. Sharrock, 'Biasing the News: Technical Issues in "Media Studies"', *Sociology*, Vol. 13, No. 3, September 1979; Graham Murdock, 'Misrepresenting Media Sociology: A Reply to Anderson and Sharrock', *Sociology*, Vol. 14, No. 3, August 1980; N. McKeganey and B. Smith, 'Reading and Writing in Collaborative Production: Some Comments Upon Anderson and Sharrock's "Biasing the News"', *Sociology*, Vol. 14, No. 4, November 1980, and W.W. Sharrock & Digby C. Anderson, 'The Persistent Evasion of Technical Issues in Media Studies', *Sociology*, Vol. 16, No. 1, February 1982.

6   See, *inter alia*, Harold Garfinkel, *Studies in Ethnomethodology* (Polity Press, Oxford, 1984); John Heritage, *Garfinkel and Ethnomethodology* (Polity Press, Oxford, 1984), J.M. Atkinson and J. Heritage (eds), *Structures of Social Action* (Cambridge University Press, Cambridge, 1984), Douglas Benson and John A. Hughes, *The Perspective of Ethnomethodology* (Longmans, N.Y., 1983); and Melvin Pollner, *Mundane Reason: Reality in Everyday and Sociological Discourse* (Cambridge University Press, Cambridge, 1987).

7   For sociology, cf. Peter Berger and Thomas Luckmann's classic text, *The Social Construction of Reality* (Doubleday, N.Y., 1966); for philosophy/ethnomethodology, see my *The Social Construction of Mind* (Macmillan, London, 1978); for social psychology, see Kenneth Gergen's statement, 'The Social Constructionist Movement in Modern Psychology', *American Psychologist*, Vol. 40, 1985; K. Gergen and K. Davis (eds), *The Social Construction of the Person* (Springer-Verlag, N.Y., 1985); and for psychology, see Rom Harré, *Personal Being: A Theory for Individual Psychology* (Basil Blackwell, Oxford, 1984).

8   For some of the classic early statements in cognitive anthropology, see Stephen Tyler (ed.), *Cognitive Anthropology* (Holt, Rinehart & Winston, 1969).

9   For a (non-representative) sample of this burgeoning field, see John Haugeland (ed.), *Mind Design* (MIT Press, Cambridge, Mass., 1981); Donald A. Norman (ed.), *Perspectives on Cognitive Science* (Ablex, Norwood, 1981); Jerry Fodor, *Representations: Philosophical Essays on the Foundations of Cognitive Science* (MIT Press, Cambridge, Mass., 1983); John Searle, *Minds, Brains and Science* (British Broadcasting Corporation, London, 1984); and, for a useful selection of debate and discussion papers, G.N. Gilbert and C. Heath (eds),

Social Action and Artificial Intelligence (Gower Press, Nottingham, 1984).

10 Peter Berger and Thomas Luckmann, *The Social Construction of Reality* (Allen Lane, London, 1967), p. 15.

11 Ibid.

12 Harold Garfinkel, 'A Conception of, and Experiments with, "Trust" as a Condition of Stable Concerted Action'. In O.J. Harvey (ed.), *Motivation and Social Interaction* (Ronald Press, N.Y., 1963) p. 236.

13 A. Schutz, *Collected Papers, Vol. 1: The Problem of Social Reality*, ed. M. Natanson (Nijhoff, The Hague, 1962).

14 Ibid., p. 10.

15 Ibid., p. 53. For useful early discussions of the relevance of Schutz to the reconstruction of the sociology of knowledge, see Matthew Speier, 'Phenomenology and Social Theory: Discovering Actors and Social Acts', *Berkeley Journal of Sociology*, 1967; and John Heeren, 'Alfred Schutz and the Sociology of Commonsense Knowledge'. In Jack D. Douglas (ed.), *Understanding Everyday Life: Toward the Reconstruction of Sociological Knowledge* (Aldine, Chicago, 1970), chapter 2.

16 For an assessment of some traditional difficulties involved in specifying the form of the relation obtaining between beliefs and actions, see, *inter alia*, Alasdair McIntyre, 'A Mistake About Causality in Social Science'. In P. Laslett and W. G. Runciman (eds), *Philosophy, Politics and Society*, 2nd Series (Basil Blackwell, Oxford, 1964) which, for all of its oversimplifications of the Weberian thesis about the relation between Protestantism and capitalist economic activity, nonetheless articulates the basic issue sharply and develops a concept of a 'practical syllogistic' relation as an (idealized) specification of the grammatical (logical) ties between assignable beliefs and assignable action-types.

17 Schutz, *collected papers.*, 1962, p. 5.

18 Peter Winch, *The Idea of a Social Science and Its Relation to Philosophy* (Routledge & Kegan Paul, London, 1958), p. 128.

19 Harold Garfinkel, *Studies in Ethnomethodology* (Prentice-Hall, N.J., 1967), p. 1.

20 Michael Mulkay, *Science and the Sociology of Knowledge* (George Allen & Unwin, London, 1979), chapter 1.

21 Karl Popper, *The Logic of Scientific Discovery* (Harper & Row, N.Y., 1959) and *Conjectures and Refutations* (Routledge & Kegan Paul, London, 1963).

22 Thomas S. Kuhn, *The Structure of Scientific Revolutions* (University of Chicago Press, Chicago, 1962).

23 See Ludwig Wittgenstein, *Philosophical Investigations* trans. G.E.M. Anscombe (Basil Blackwell, Oxford, 1953). For some useful discussion of the notion of 'autonomy of grammar', see G. Baker and P.M.S.

Hacker, *Wittgenstein on Rules, Grammar and Necessity* (Vol. 2 of *Analytical Commentary on the Philosophical Investigations*) (University of Chicago Press, Chicago, 1984).

24 For example, see H.M. Collins, 'The Seven Sexes: A Study in the Sociology of a Phenomenon, or the Replication of Experiment in Physics', *Sociology*, Vol. 9, 1975.

25 See G.N. Gilbert, 'The Transformation of Research Findings into Scientific Knowledge', *Social Studies of Science*, Vol. 6, 1976.

26 See G.N. Gilbert and M. Mulkay, 'Warranting Scientific Belief', *Social Studies of Science*, Vol. 12, 1982.

27 G.N. Gilbert and M. Mulkay, *Opening Pandora's Box: An Analysis of Scientists' Discourse* (Cambridge University Press, Cambridge, 1984).

28 Harold Garfinkel, Michael Lynch and Eric Livingston, 'The Work of a Discovering Science Construed with Materials from the Optically Discovered Pulsar', *Philosophy of the Social Sciences*, Vol. 11, 1981.

29 B. Latour and S. Woolgar, *Laboratory Life: The Social Construction of Scientific Facts* (Sage, London, 1979).

30 See Augustine Brannigan, *The Social Basis of Scientific Discoveries* (Cambridge University Press, Cambridge, 1981). For a discussion of modes of *de*-legitimation in science, see Harry M. Collins and Trevor Pinch, *Frames of Meaning: The Social Construction of Extraordinary Science* (Routledge & Kegan Paul, London, 1982).

31 Garfinkel, *Studies in Ethnomethodology*, p. 77.

32 Gilbert Ryle, *The Concept of Mind* (Hutchinson, London, 1949), chapter 2.

33 Michael Polanyi, *Personal Knowledge* (Routledge & Kegan Paul, London, 1958).

34 Noam Chomsky, *Aspects of the Theory of Syntax* (MIT Press, Cambridge, Mass., 1965), p. 4.

35 For an extensive critique of Chomsky's mentalism and neural representationism, see G.P. Baker and P.M.S. Hacker, *Language, Sense and Nonsense* (Basil Blackwell, Oxford, 1984), chapters 7–10.

36 J.L. Austin, *How To Do Things With Words*, ed. J.O. Urmson (Oxford University Press, N.Y., 1962): John Searle, *Speech Acts* (Cambridge University Press, Cambridge, 1969).

37 See Tyler (ed.), *Cognitive Anthropology*.

38 See, *inter alia*, Charles O. Frake, 'The Ethnographic Study of Cognitive Systems'. In *Anthropology and Human Behavior* (Anthropological Society of Washington, Washington D.C. 1962); and his 'Notes on Queries in Ethnography', *American Anthropologist*, Vol. 66, No. 3, Part 2, June 1964.

39 For some useful compendia of conversation-analytic studies, see Jim Schenkein (ed.), *Studies in the Organization of Conversational*

Interaction (Academic Press, N.Y., 1978); J.M. Atkinson and J. Heritage (eds), *Structures of Social Action: Studies in Conversation Analysis* (Cambridge University Press, Cambridge, 1984); and G. Button, P. Drew and J. Heritage (eds), 'Interaction and Language Use', Special Issue of *Human Studies*, Vol. 9, Nos 2–3, 1986.

40   Berger and Luckmann, *Social Construction of Reality*, pp. 52, 56.

41   H. Garfinkel, 'Good Organisational Reasons for "Bad" Clinic Records', in his *Studies in Ethnomethodology*, chapter 6.

42   Aaron Cicourel, 'Police Practices and Official Records'. In Roy Turner (ed.), *Ethnomethodology* (Penguin, London, 1974), chapter 8: extracted from Cicourel's The Social Organisation of Juvenile Justice (Wiley, N.Y., 1968), pp. 112–323.

43   Don Zimmerman, 'Fact as a Practical Accomplishment'. In Turner (ed.), *Ethnomethodology*, Chapter 12.

44   George Psathas, 'Organisational Features of Direction Maps'. In his edited collection, *Everyday Language: Studies in Ethnomethodology* (Irvington Press, N.Y., 1979).

45   Dorothy Smith, 'The Social Construction of Documentary Reality', *Sociological Inquiry*, Vol. 44, No. 4, 1974.

46   John O'Neill, 'The Literary Production of Natural and Social Science Inquiry', *Canadian Journal of Sociology*, Vol. 6, 1981.

47   Michael Lynch, 'Discipline and the Material Form of Images: An Analysis of Scientific Visibility', *Social Studies of Science*, Vol. 15, 1985.

48   Lena Jayyusi, 'Toward a Socio-Logic of the Filmic Text', *Semiotica*, Vol. 68, Nos. 3/4.

49   Ludwig Wittgenstein, *Philosophical Investigations*, trans. G.E.M. Anscombe (Basil Blackwell, Oxford, 1968), paras 202–311. For an excellent commentary, see P.M.S. Hacker, *Insight and Illusion: Themes in the Philosophy of Wittgenstein* (Revised ed., Clarendon Press, Oxford, 1986), chapters 9–11.

2

The Socio-Logic of Knowledge and Belief

A good deal of contemporary research and theorizing in this area has turned our attention away from 'ideology-critique' and what Bloor has felicitously termed the 'sociology of error'.[1] Among the traditional themes examined under such auspices had been the question of the 'irrationality' or otherwise of magic and oracular practices in some African cultures,[2] the general sociohistorical analysis and critique of many of the major political 'ideologies' of our times (e.g. nationalism, capitalism, etc.)[3] and the exposé of 'standard' psychiatric epistemologies arising out of the critical sociology of mental illness.[4]

While asserting an analytical interest in the logic of social cognition and conduct which facilitates the construction of truths (as well as falsehoods), rational (as well as irrational) outcomes, correct (as well as incorrect) results, conforming (as well as deviant) productions, we do not have to embrace such assessments explicitly ourselves *as analysts*. It is sufficient for our *socio-logical* purposes to bracket the ultimate epistemic status of whatever piece of knowledge we are interested in exploring by conceptualizing such knowledge to consist in currently ratified knowledge-claim(s) (some of which may well have defeasible and corrigible aspects). Such a methodological device is not, as some commentators have appeared to believe, an abdication of responsibility: it is, rather, a product both of a strong sense of the limitations of the social scientist in his capacity to make such adjudications unilaterally and absolutely and of the restricted relevances of his analytical focus. Does this mean that we are, willy-nilly, committed to relativism?

Whatever the demerits of the philosophical thesis of the relativity of truth, the only 'relativity' necessarily embraced by the epistemic sociologist is the (perhaps anemic) one of 'relativity' to (social, cultural) forms of conceptualization and conduct domains. Just as there can be no 'truths' communicable – even 'thinkable' – independently of the conceptual resources necessary for their articulation, so also can there be no 'truths' determinable as such independently of human purposes and courses of action. A claim such as: 'The sun rose this morning' made for example by a child in the construction of an English composition about his observations of the day's events, is no more 'falsified' or 'rendered untrue' in the light of the astronomically ascertained 'facticity' of the relative motion of earth and sun (*pace* Jarvie) than is a claim about the 'exact' length of a table given in feet and inches refuted by a measurement operation carried out elsewhere, for different purposes, by a micro-measurement instrument capable of micron calibration.[5] Furthermore, while the proposition that 'the earth is round' may receive near-universal assent as a general observational claim in most technically developed societies (which assent alone is no guarantor of its truth), its *demonstrability* (to e.g. cultural neophytes) requires a good deal of argument and background knowledge (such as the elementary reference of the category 'earth' being a planetary body, the truth of the claim that someone traveling from any given point on the earth's surface will return to that point if continuing unimpeded in a given direction, the facticity of space travel, the reliability of photographic representations, etc.). Here, we must note a distinction between what could be called '*theory*-laden truth-claims' (such as 'the rate of change of the temperature of a gas is directly proportional to the rate of change of its volume and pressure') and '*concept*-laden truth-claims' which may or may not enter into the construction of some theoretical scheme (such as 'salt dissolves in water'). The former depend upon the (successful) elaboration of a theoretical framework, whereas the latter are contingent upon observation and elementary, non-technical kinds of conceptualization. And then we encounter the 'factual' claims which Wittgenstein terms 'hinge' propositions,[6] such as 'my name is JC', 'here is one hand – my own', 'the earth has existed during the last five minutes', which lack the same demonstrability criteria and whose indubitability is of a very different kind from that of the proposition about the earth's rotundity. With these examples, we have barely scratched the surface of the more esoteric constructions of (institutionalized) knowledge-production arrangements (e.g. electrostatic researches developing from the production of Coulomb's law; the development of proofs for Euler's theorems; the derivation by microbiological theorists of the model of the DNA molecule, or the refutation of Lamarckian genetic principles, to name but a few of those better known to our own culture).

The cultural-conceptual and praxiological[7] foundations, and reproduceably intersubjective demonstrations, of such claims to knowledge as these testify to their 'relativity' in the terms which interest us for our analytical purposes: their dependent relationships to communication and conceptualization, instrumental and practical social conduct. They are 'cultural' products, not in the sense that their validity 'varies with culture' (unless that highly misleading phrase is taken to mean that the *assignment* of validity to them is a function of certain cultural prerequisites which may not be universally shared across the human species), but in the sense that specific forms of cultural organization made them possible and facilitate their reproduction as epistemic phenomena.

According to one prominent conception of inquiry into (scientific) knowledge(-claims), however, our interest should be directed to providing essentially *causal* explanations of their origins within society.

Knowledge-Claims and Social 'Causation'

In what Bloor terms the 'strong programme' in the sociology of knowledge, with its clear indebtedness to Durkheim's classical causal sociology, analysts are enjoined to search for 'laws' governing the production of (scientific, but also other types of) knowledge. Bloor states four principles of inquiry for the 'strong programme':

1. It would be causal, that is, concerned with the conditions which would bring about belief or states of knowledge. Naturally there will be other types of causes apart from social ones which will cooperate in bringing about belief.
2. It would be impartial with respect to truth and falsity, rationality or irrationality, success or failure. Both sides of these dichotomies will require explanation.

3. It would be symmetrical in its style of explanation. The same types of cause would explain, say, true and false beliefs.

4. It would be reflexive. In principle its patterns of explanation would have to be applicable to sociology itself . . .[8]

These precepts have engendered a good deal of debate in the field;[9] a full adjudication of them would require an assessment of the Durkheimian programme in general.[10] I shall restrict myself to a consideration of its proposal of a causal-explanatory mode of inquiry for knowledge and belief, since I seek to make a sharp distinction between the 'strong programme' and those styles of investigation which could be termed 'logical' or 'praxiological' in epistemic sociology.

A first question would be: in what sense can sociologists 'explain' the beliefs or knowledge-claims of members? They might simply decide to catalogue members' own answers to questions such as: 'How did you come to believe X?', or 'What convinced you of the truth (correctness, rationality) of Y?' Here, they would be gathering agents' 'reasons' for holding the beliefs or making the claims they do: in proceeding this way, the sociologist would admit into his collection of 'agents' explanatory accounts' only those which 'made sense' – that is, which could be seen as in some way(s) rationally related to the beliefs and/or knowledge-claims under scrutiny *according to the sociologist*. After all, someone may hold a belief and yet give a surprisingly idiosyncratic or bizarre reason for holding it; it may, indeed, not be acceptable *as a reason* at all by some standards. But *whose* standards? Is the sociologist simply to be a members' mouthpiece (in McHugh's pointed terminology)? If so, what is *his* distinctive contribution to the explanation of members' claims? If not, what criteria can be introduced to govern the specification of what is said by a member as a cataloguable 'explanation' of his belief or knowledge-claim? How are such criteria to be justified generically so as to ensure coding consistency across the catalogue? And what purposes of generalization could be served by a catalogue of possibly very varied, contextually-grounded answers to the kinds of question we indicated might be asked? Giving reasons for beliefs is *itself* a mode of practical conduct, tied to conventions, purposes and local contextual particulars of various kinds. Characteristically, a sociologist who seeks to extrapolate from a set of 'members' explanations' some generic explanatory 'core', 'essence' or 'principle(s)' will be engaged in radical decontextualization as well as unilateral adequacy assessment. It is preferable, as a methodological procedure, to study reasons and the giving of them as themselves part of the phenomena to be investigated – epistemic conduct – rather than as bases for quasi-transcendental explanations-in-general.

What, then, becomes of the goal of *sociological* explanation in this domain? Would a search for 'causes' fare better? At least, it would appear, it would enable an investigator to transcend agents' various, situated reasons and posit conditions perhaps (indeed, preferably) either unknown to agents themselves or at least not discursively known to them. This, as may be remembered, was Durkheim's hope in by-passing suicide notes as potential explanations of suicides in favor of causal, 'suicidogenic' variables in the social circumstances of (categories of) persons who committed suicide. For Bloor and others who share his program, the sociologist dealing with epistemic phenomena should search out 'conditions which would bring about belief or states of knowledge' irrespective of 'truth or falsity',[11] although it should be noted here that according to some 'belief' the status of 'a state of *knowledge*' is *eo ipso* to accord to it the status of 'true'. (Thus, in the very initial characterization of the phenomenon as either a 'belief' or an item of 'knowledge', a decision has been made as between the 'truth' or (possible) 'falsity' of the claim, thus contravening the initial aspiration to preserve 'impartiality'.) What could count as conditions which would 'bring about' beliefs or knowledge-claims beyond those acknowledged by agents themselves as circumstances or considerations which were sufficient to be *convincing* to them? For something to 'bring about' the holding of a belief or the serious articulation of a sincere knowledge-claim, it would (logically) have to qualify as a 'convincing ground' for the agent. We do not (properly) say of something that it 'caused us to' or 'made us' *believe* something (to be true) unless it figured as a wholly persuasive or decisive consideration in our reasoning: how then could conditions *not* known to or entertained by agents be counted as compelling (coercive, 'causal') bases for their having the beliefs they have? Some of the beliefs which people acquire are acquired by their being taught them explicitly without the provision of grounds: as Wittgenstein put it, 'The child learns by believing the adult. Doubt comes *after* belief. I learned an enormous amount and accepted it on human authority, and then I found some things confirmed or disconfirmed by my own experience.'[12] Just as doubt comes after belief in many cases, so also may the provision of, or the giving of, reasons for believing. Yet it is hardly a sociological insight to count 'teaching' or 'parental (or other determinable sources of) authority' as 'causes' of beliefs. Beliefs acquired like this may well be *inculcated*, but not caused. It is to stretch the meaning of 'cause' out of shape to use it in such contexts, especially if, as Bloor seeks to argue, we are to speak the nomological language of causation (i.e. of causal *laws*) in so doing. Of course, there are conditions which might be specified that are necessary (although hardly *sufficient*) for the having of certain beliefs and the formation of certain knowledge-claims, and one may attempt to specify correlations between certain sorts of social arrangement (economic interests, levels of industrialization, levels of education, religious affiliations, positions in status hierarchies, relationships within information networks, etc.) and the holding of certain beliefs, but once again we are a long way from 'causal explanation(s)' of their genesis or fixation. It is a prerequisite of my being able to walk that I have legs or their prosthetic equivalents, but the having of them does not necessitate or cause my walking when(ever) I do so: my behavior in walking may co-vary exactly with the availability of other forms of transportation and some calculable set of desti-nations to which I must travel, but neither the lack of availability of alternative transportation other than my legs nor the nature of my destination 'bring it about that' I walk. I may send someone else, decide it is too far to go to achieve some objective or too much of a hassle, or select any number of other options open to me in such circumstances. To continue the analogy, no matter how many variables are factored into a multiple regression in such a case, it is never true that, given such variables' obtaining, one would have *no choice but to* walk! Maybe a gun pointed to my head in connection with a command to walk, or the presence of dire personal or familial danger, would 'cause me to walk', but here the causality is not the nomological causality of the physical sciences but the commonplace 'causality' of *compelling reasons* (and justifying ones at that). The case of beliefs and knowledge-claims is even further distant from such a paradigm: no life-threatening circumstance nor any amount of direct physical coercion, which, in the case of walking and many other actions may be normatively characterized as 'leaving one with no option', 'giving one no alternative', or 'giving one no choice but to . . .', could figure as a necessitation of a 'belief'. It may be *rational*, under such circumstances as a dire physical threat, to believe that one's life is in danger, but one cannot be *forced to believe*, for example, that the President is a liar or that chlorophyll is necessary to photosynthesis, by being threatened with harm if one does not, however eagerly one may utter the relevant words!

The 'causal-explanatory' program in the area of epistemic phenomena such as beliefs and knowledge-claims, then, is merely a rhetorical gloss for an enterprise in which various (socio-historical) preconditions are to be sought for the genesis, dissemination and acceptance/rejection of beliefs and related phenomena of interest. It is, however, misleading in its claim to '*explain*' beliefs. Moreover, it detracts attention from the very issue which motivated the programme in the first place − an interest in the *content* of (scientific and other) knowledge-claims as social phenomena. For this interest, we need to reveal, not the putative 'causes' or conditions unknown to agents, but the *logic* of agents' actual conceptual, communicative, relational and instrumental conduct as they constitute their object-universes.[13]

The intelligibility of any sociocultural and physical environment, its personnel and their activities, its objects and situations, its history and prospects, is contingent both upon the background knowledge and beliefs of its participant agents. To illustrate these themes, let us consider two topics of inquiry: the organization of socially conventionalized background knowledge and the role of beliefs in members' orientations to the world. In exploring these topics, we can begin more adequately to display some aspects of the logic of inquiry of a sociology of cognition of the kind we have been characterizing programmatically.

Knowledge and Belief: The Logic of Members' Resources

One basic theoretical interest in the field has been to analyse how members of a social collectivity may be said by others to know or to believe whatever it is that they know or believe, and this interest was motivated in part by an attempt to come to terms with the 'problem of imputation'[14] recast as a problem of *practical* rather than theoretical reason in the first instance.

In his account of the classical problem of imputation, Barnes states:

Whether and how thought or belief can be attributed to social class, or other (social) formations, as the consequences of their particular interests, constitutes the problem of imputation in the sociology of knowledge. . . . Despite wide-ranging disagreements upon what constituted a class, its interests and its beliefs, all investigators were able to agree that simple direct correspondence between these various entities as empirical phenomena could not convincingly be established. Beliefs which seemed rationally indicated by the interests of one class were found to be disturbingly common among the members of another . . . sometimes so much diversity of belief and thought was found within a class as to preclude analysis of what were the dominant forms . . . . On the other hand, it was still reasonable, on the basis of what had been empirically revealed, to hold that some relationship existed between beliefs, interests and social structure.[15]

However, in Sharrock's terms,

The problem for sociologists has not been . . . that of interpreting the relationship between a collectivity's corpus of knowledge and the activities of its members [but] how do we come, in the very first place, to conceive of a corpus of knowledge as a *collectivity's* corpus? To suppose that a connection can be made between a collectivity's corpus and its members' activities is to presuppose that there is already such a relationship between the corpus of knowledge and the social structure as will permit the ascription of the corpus to one or another collectivity.'[16]

If, for example, research indicates that a range of beliefs characterizable as constituting 'bourgeois ideology' are to be found espoused by many (but *how* many?) members of the 'proletariat', what is the warrant for referring to such beliefs as 'bourgeois'? Sharrock's insight is to deny that the attribution of a collectivity's name to a corpus of knowledge or belief could be a matter of an attribution of *empirical scope of subscription* (e.g. that 'Roman law' is a set of legal precepts peculiar to all and only all of the members of Roman society), and to affirm instead that the use of the name of a collectivity, when describing a corpus of knowledge/belief, signals a relationship of *ownership* rather than empirical, quantitative distribution.

Sharrock observes:

Once the corpus of knowledge has been given a name, then, that name is used as a device-for-describing and *cannot thus be construed as being*

*literally descriptive of the constituency within which the corpus has
currency*. Does this mean that there is after all no connection between corpus
and collectivity, that the name in common is merely coincidentally held? The
idea that the name is intended as literally descriptive is mistaken. The name is
never intended to describe the persons amongst whom the corpus has
currency but, instead, to specify the relationship which that corpus has to the
constituency, a relationship which seems analogous to that of ownership.
Thus the naming of a corpus of knowledge as Baka medicine does not imply
that that medicine is known only to the Baka but, rather, that such medicine
in some sense 'belongs' to them, can be seen to be 'owned' by them.[17]
(emphasis added)

If persons categorizable as 'Azande' begin to practise 'Baka
medicine', it does not thereby become 'Azande medicine' but, rather,
a case of Azande practising 'Baka medicine'. When the British took
over the institutions of Roman law, it did not thereby, automatically,
become 'British' law – such a development took a great deal of time
and experience in the use of, and proprietary attitude towards,
hitherto Roman law. However, as Jayyusi observes,[18]

Not only does the medicine in Sharrock's example not come to be known as
Azande medicine, but neither do its Azande practitioners come to be known
as Baka persons. This indicates the following distinction which Sharrock
overlooks (in part because all the examples he gives derive from one class of
collectivities, namely ethnic ones).
  The practice of Baka medicine (or thought, law, religion) by non-Bakas
does *not* expand the constituency of that collectivity – but for collectivities
such as Christians, Marxists, etc., as in Christian ritual, Marxist materialism, the practice of or subscription to the corpus of knowledge/belief
constitutes the membership of that collectivity. The collectivity is expanded
if and when non-Christians or non-Marxists take up, come to believe or
subscribe to Christian or Marxist thought and/or practice. Note that the
relationship of 'ownership' still holds, but there is a consequential difference
that is displayed in the way these different sort of category-concepts may be
said to behave.[19]

We can begin, in this discussion, to see how *categories of social
membership* and their 'grammars' of application are significantly
bound up with our everyday, practical appreciation of the distribution of knowledge and belief, and how a mistaken conception of
the relationship between a collectivity-category and a category
which names a corpus of knowledge/belief could have led to a
conceptual quandry in the traditional sociology of knowledge.

It was Harvey Sacks who introduced sociologists to the idea of a logic or grammar for membership categories, and who proposed that the use of such categories enables members of a communication community to make warrantable inferences, judgements and attributions with respect to 'who knows what'.[20] It is instructive to consider an example in some detail here.

Let us take that subset of the total set of categories available for designating social identity which Sacks termed 'Standardized Relational Pairs'. These include such linked pairs of categories as 'friend–friend', 'boyfriend–girlfriend', 'neighbor–neighbor', 'parent–child', 'brother–sister', 'husband–wife', 'stranger–stranger', and the like.[21] Sacks remarks that, although such categories are elementary, the organization of knowledge which their use provides for is complex. A minimal specification of that organization is given in the following:

1) If any Member X knows his own pair position with respect to some Member Y, [e.g. if someone knows that he can properly be categorized as a 'boyfriend' of a particular person] then X knows the pair position of Y with respect to himself. [E.g. he knows that that person may correctly be categorized as his 'girlfriend'.] X also knows that if Y knows what pair position Y has to X, then Y knows what pair position X has to Y.
2) If any Member Z (neither X nor Y) knows what X takes to be X's pair position to Y, then Z knows what pair position X takes it that Y has to X. Z also knows that X takes it that if Y knows that X stands to Y in the pair position X supposes, then Y takes it that Y stands to X in the pair position X supposes. Z knows too that the converse holds for Y. Z knows further, as X and Y know, what the rights and obligations are that obtain between X and Y given a convergence in their determination of their respective pair positions.[22]

A good deal of ordinary knowledge, then, may be said to be categorially-bound. In particular, many activity-types may be said to be *bound* to particular membership categories such that, in Sacks' formulation, 'for an observer of a category-bound activity the category to which the activity is bound has a special relevance for formulating an identification of its doer'[23]. Given knowledge of *either* the contextually-relevant category-auspices of a member *or* the nature of the activity being performed, one can, for category-bound activities, 'tell' either what kinds of thing such a member can be found to be doing or who the member is. Thus, although someone engaged in 'electing a candidate' may *correctly* be categorizable as a 'veteran', a 'bookworm', a 'socialite' or a 'husband', the activity-type is categorially bound to the category 'voter', such that it is 'voters', *not* 'husbands', who 'elect': similarly, 'sentencing' is bound to 'judge', 'firing' to 'employer', 'diagnosing a physical illness' to 'doctor', 'arresting' to 'police', and so on. (Note that by 'bound' one does not assert a relationship between category and activity such that the activity is bound to all and only all of the incumbents of a given category.)

Descriptions of agents and their activities are characteristically co-selected to exhibit an orientation to category-boundedness considerations. Sacks observes that, in coming across a scene in which someone is crying, where that person cannot be seen to be an adult, then, 'without respect to the fact that it is a baby, it could be either "male" or "female", and nonetheless I would not, and I take it you would not, seeing the scene, see that "a male cried" if we could see that "a baby cried"'.[24]

Beliefs, also, may be construed as categorially organized for certain purposes. Consider the following alternative reports upon an event: (i) 'The city councilmen refused the demonstrators a permit because they feared violence' and (ii) 'The city councilmen refused the demonstrators a permit because they advocated revolution'. To whom is it most natural to assume that the pronoun 'they' refers in each report? Given the conventionalized distribution of beliefs to categories in our culture, we may be more likely to take 'they' in report (i) as a transformation of 'councilmen', and in report (ii) as a transformation of 'demonstrators':[25] pushed to its extremes, such categorially predicated assignations of belief can become stereotyping, prejudicial or racist, although it is clear that our knowledge and experience is organised to a significant degree by such *structured inferential affordances*[26] of the use of membership categories.

It has often been argued that 'our beliefs shape our perceptions' just as significantly as our knowledge. However, 'seeing' and 'hearing' are quite different modalities in respect of their relationships to 'knowledge' and 'belief'. Certainly, it is generally true to say that how we may hear various things which are said to us, or read various things which are written for us, is a function of the beliefs we have as well as the knowledge we possess. And beliefs are subject to social systematization, which is what enables us to design what we say and write knowing how it can be heard and read by anonymous others whose repertoire of 'possible beliefs' we can rely on, even when their actual beliefs may be variously related to that conventionalized range. It is worth noting here, however, that whereas 'hear(ing) that X' does not presuppose that X is known, 'see(ing) that X' does presuppose X. In other words, seeing-that is 'factive' (i.e. presupposes the *truth* of its object-complement), while hearing-that (such-and-such happened) is non-factive. If I heard that you were ill, you may none the less not have been ill, but if I saw that you were ill, then it follows that you *were* ill – otherwise I could only be credited with seeing you *and thinking that* you were ill.

Let us, then, consider *seeing* things and failing to see them, seeing that things are thus-and-so or wholly otherwise, and seeing samenesses and differences, similarities and dissimilarities in things. How do 'beliefs' figure in these achievements?

Most of us, for example, cannot see ghosts, whereas some of us can – or, at least, claim that we can. Alien beings, fairies, ectoplasm, levitations, divine healings, and a host of other phenomena which (apparently) populate the world for, *inter alia*, children, members of religious sects, mental patients, etc., are simply not visible for the rest of us. Yet those who (claim to) see such things rarely get away with accusing the rest of us of defective visual capacities, and we who do not (claim to) see such things rarely ascribe extraordinary optical powers to those who do. As Pollner has so eloquently analysed these issues,[27] the management of discrepant perceptual claims embroils a range of options, and can take on the character of a political struggle over a *fundamental* equivocality. He considers the example of one party's claim to have 'heard voices' confronting another party's claim that he did not hear them at all. The latter accuses the former of 'hearing things', whilst the former accuses the latter of being 'hard of hearing'.

Which of these alternate solutions is appropriate, however, turns on whether or not the voices were 'really' available for the hearing. But of course, whether or not the voices are actually present is precisely the problematic which precipitates the search for a resolution in the first place. The solution of the puzzle posed by the disjunctive hearings requires a decision as to whether there was a voice to be heard. Yet whether there was a voice to be heard is the very issue comprising the disjuncture . . . . We learn from the presence of these potentially endless equivocalities that resolution of reality disjunctures cannot simply be achieved by 'looking' at the world.'[28]

Thus, we have the 'political' management of discrepant claims about percepts in which 'relativization to belief' figures as one method for sustaining one side of a disjuncture *at the expense of the other*. If I fail to see the ghost you see, and I claim that your 'perception' was purely a product of your 'believing in ghosts', you can retort that you do not 'merely believe', but rather you *know* that there are such things because (perhaps among other reasons) you just saw one! What, after all, did Joan of Arc see? A 'divine vision' or an 'hallucination'? A method for defeating, denying or degrading someone's perceptual claim, then, is to assign to it the status of having been a function of mere 'belief'.

Beliefs, then, are certainly invoked in accounting for *discrepant* perceptual claims of various kinds. But do beliefs enable us to *see* things-in-common? I shall argue that the answer to this question is *no*. A belief, at least of a declarative or propositional kind, is a *guarded* claim about something. To say of myself or of someone else that I/he 'believe(s)' that X, or in the existence of X, or something about X, is to *refrain from* espousing a knowledge-claim. (I shall leave aside the limiting case of theological claims here, in which an avowal of 'belief in God' conventionally *lacks* these properties of uncertainty, guardedness or doubt.) A perceptual claim, however, presupposes a claim to facticity, to knowledge. A claim to 'perceive', to 'see', and to 'observe' may be *contrasted* to a claim to '*seem* to perceive', '*seem* to see', '*believe that* one saw', '*think that* one sees', '*apparently* to observe', and the like. To perceive X is for X to exist: to believe that, or to think that, one perceives X is to *withhold* the existential or 'factive' commitment logically entailed by its *un*guarded use. Perception is an achievement: *apparently* perceiving, being logically compatible with misperceiving or not perceiving, has no such status. Thus, while knowledge can constitute what is perceived, belief cannot. And it is futile to propose that 'knowledge is, after all, true belief'. Knowledge is not 'true belief'. If I cease to know something, then I have forgotten it: if I cease to believe something that is true, I have not, thereby, forgotten it.[29] I can be asked: 'How do you know?' but I cannot be asked: 'How do you believe?' I can be asked: 'Why do you believe that?' but not: 'Why do you know that?' To sum up: the avowal or ratified ascription of belief cannot be appealed to as a criterion for a claim to see; at best, it can be a criterion for a claim to 'seem to see'. Those who claim knowledge of X may, in appropriate contexts, legitimately claim perception of X. Those (with the now conventionalized theological exception) who claim only to believe X cannot claim thereby to perceive X.

Surely, however, it can be argued that 'beliefs structure perception' in the domain of 'illusion'? I want to argue that this is not so, although this will require extended discussion. Consider the famous Müller-Lyer illusion:

Here, one would ordinarily say that the top line looks longer – even that it *is* longer – than the bottom line, whether or not one knows the actual length of the lines (which are, in fact, exactly equal). If one claimed to *see that* the top line was longer, this claim would have to be withdrawn in favor of one of seeing it *as* (if it were) longer when the nature of the illusion is indicated. However, once it is demonstrated that both lines are of equal length, one *still* says that one sees the top line as longer than the bottom one. Whereas one now has to say that he *believed that* the top line was longer, but now *knows* it to be of equal length, and thus can no longer claim to *see that* it is longer as one did prior to the disclosure of its having the same length, none the less this transition from former belief to present knowledge of the length of the lines does *not* entail a transition to *seeing that* both lines have the same length, or to *seeing* the equal length of both lines! Contrast this case to a different one of a transition from belief to knowledge in respect of a perceptual object. Let us suppose that you suddenly claim to (be able to) see someone crouching in the shadows, but on closer inspection or by virtue of someone's disclosure it turns out to be an old sack. You must consequently transform *both* the description of the object of your orientation and the characterization of your perceptual act or achievement.

You must now say something like: 'Whereas before I *thought (believed) I could see* someone crouching in the shadows, now I *see that* it is an only a sack. Thus, I did *not* see someone crouching there, because no one was there to be seen, but only *thought that I saw* someone.' In the case of the Muller-Lyer illusion, the transition from (mistaken) belief to knowledge does not ordinarily or necessarily affect the characterization in the same way. One does *not* have to say: 'Whereas before I *thought I saw* the top line as longer than the bottom one, now I can *see that* they are the same length.' Ordinarily, even subsequent to the disclosure of the lines' equal lengths, one still does not (unless using rulers as one looks) *see that* they are so. What distinguishes the case of the transition from belief to knowledge in respect of such an illusion from other instances of transitions from belief to knowledge in the domain of perception is this: one's acquired knowledge does not affect how one can still characterize one's perceptual claim. One may still claim *not to be able to see that* the lines are of equal length as one looks at them, even though one knows that they are. But one can only rationally characterize one's perceptual claim in terms of '*seeming to see*' that the lines are of different lengths. Thus, illusions such as this, while affording an interesting variation from the modes of depiction otherwise characteristic of belief-to-knowledge transitions in the domain of perception, still do not warrant the assertion that 'beliefs structure perception'. At best, beliefs inform '*apparent* perception(s)'.

In his account of transformations in knowledge-claims in science, Kuhn argued that paradigm changes 'cause scientists to see the world of their research-engagement differently. In so far as their only recourse to that world is through what they see and do, we may want to say that after a (scientific) revolution scientists are responding to a different world.'[30] Although such a conception of what is involved understates the role of a common, pre-theoretical natural language within which communication can proceed (however cumbersomely) and with which scientists can reason to some degree independently of their paradigmatic commitments, Kuhn's discussion alerts us to the particular problems involved in considering the historicity of concept-formation. 'When Aristotle and Galileo looked at swinging stones, the first saw constrained fall, the second a pendulum.'[31] These different conceptualizations of the objects of perception grammatically constrained the kind of measurements and laws of motion which could be contemplated by each perceiver. Note, however, that *theory*-ladenness enters only after the initial pre-theoretical conceptualization of the object as a 'swinging stone'. The 'truth' of Galilean laws are clearly relative to the invocation of the concept of a pendulum. Does Galileo's achievement constitute an overthrow of what had previously been regarded as a 'given' truth – that swinging bodies are bodies falling with difficulty? Does it furnish support for a relativistic conception of scientific 'truth'? Does it represent, then, a 'more objective observation' of the swinging body?

The claim that 'a swinging body is falling with difficulty' (rather than a pendulum) can, in our post-Galilean world, now only be made if it is taken to presuppose *additional impediments* to its fall beyond the chain to which it is attached. We would say of a swinging body that its falling 'with difficulty' or 'under constraint' is true about it only under the condition that something *beyond the body and its attachment itself* were slowing it down or interfering with its swing (such as the introduction of an upward draft). Before Galileo and the acceptance of his framework, constrained fall would have been taken to constitute the swinging of the body itself *just in virtue of its attachment to a chain*. In this sense, the *meaning* of the expression 'a swinging body is falling with difficulty' has changed to reflect the new conventions attaching to our use of the concept of a 'pendulum'. Ullin Place gives a similar example:

Take for example the principle that whales are fishes. If we adopt the medieval definition of a fish as a creature which lives in the sea and propels itself through the water by means of fins and a characteristically paddle-shaped tail, the statement *whales are fishes* is an analytic truth, since, on that usage, the criteria for assigning an object to the class *whales* include those for assigning an object to the class *fishes*. But once we adopt the modern convention according to which a fish has to be cold-blooded and reproduce itself by means of eggs fertilised outside the body and which precludes anything that is a mammal from also being a fish, the sentence *whales are fishes* becomes an analytic falsehood. However, because of the changed conventions, the proposition which *whales are fishes* used to express, given the previous conventions, *is not the same proposition as that which the same sentence now expresses*.[32]

In this sense, then, the grammar of the expression 'a swinging body is falling with difficulty' has been changed; because of the new conventions, the proposition which it used to express, given the previous (Aristotelian) conventions, is not the same proposition which the same sentence can now express (after Galileo). (Place goes on to use this argument to counter the theory of common names as 'rigid designators' due to Kripke and others.) The crux of Place's thesis is that 'the same sentence can express a true proposition at one time and place and a false proposition at another time and place', a thesis which he construes as a form of sophisticated social relativity.[33] It is a kind of 'social relativism' in-so-far as the truth of any proposition is determined in part by the social conventions governing the words used in a sentence used to express it. But there is *no* relativism of a purely 'factual' kind: if Galileo was correct, then his laws of motion are *absolutely* true. That is, they are true not just for Galileo and his immediate historical followers, but true for us as well in the late twentieth century. Does such (transhistorical) 'absolute truth' afford us a 'more objective observation' of a swinging body than had been available to us prior to Galileo?

From where we now stand, it seems easy to make an irony out of an Aristotelian's perceptual claim about swinging bodies' falling with difficulty. We may say something like: 'When he looked at a swinging stone, he seemed to see constrained fall.' The Aristotelian, however, would have said something like: 'I see [not 'I seem to see'] constrained fall'. What, then, objectively, did the Aristotelian *actually* see? We cannot 'take his word for it' in characterizing the object of his perception, since to do so would commit us to his (pre-Galilean) conception of swinging bodies which we cannot share: but *not* to take his word for it would 'put words into his mouth' which he could not have articulated in describing the object of his perception. There appears to be no way of standing outside of our commitments in terms of contemporary knowledge-claims when we come to characterize the object of his perception, and in this sense we cannot claim to be giving a 'more objective observational description' of what *he* saw, even though we can certainly give what we would claim to be a 'more objective observational description' of *what there was to be seen*. As Pitkin notes in her discussion of Kuhn, to say about the world of a pre-Galilean that *there were no pendulums for anyone to see* is significantly to mislead: it is true that no one could have *said* that they could see a pendulum prior to Galileo, but false to say that there were no pendulums in that world.[34] There is, however, no commitment-independent way of specifying *what was there to be seen*.

Now consider the following case, drawn from Fingarette's classic study of the origins of the criminal insanity plea in the case of M'Naghten:

For though he knew that the law generally proscribes killing the prime minister and that the public generally condemns such acts, he was incapable of forming a rational moral judgment on the relation of his own particular act to law or public morality. *For it was his irrational belief* [that the Tories were persecuting him and his life was in danger] *that made his action appear as a last desperate act of self-defense*. Hence, for him [M'Naghten] the relevant definition of his act with respect to its moral aspect was 'an act of desperate self-defense' rather than 'assassination of the prime minister'. (emphasis added)[35]

Fingarette, in describing this predicament, cannot say of M'Naghten's act that it *was* 'a last desperate act of self-defense'; not sharing M'Naghten's beliefs, he must contend that they 'made his action *appear as*' an act of self-defense, thus saving the floor for the characterization of what the act *actually was*, and, thus, what it could only, rationally, have been *seen* to be. In such contexts as these, the appearance/perception dichotomy maps quite neatly onto that of belief/knowledge. Although it may well have *appeared* to M'Naghten, and to any others who may have shared his beliefs, as a desperate act of self-defense, it could only have been seen to be an assassination (attempt).

W.V. Quine developed a useful distinction between *opaque* and *transparent* contexts of reference and attribution,[36] which we can put to work in this discussion. An *opaque context* of reference/attribution is one in which a characterization of an object is given in terms of how the *subject* saw it, heard it or in some other way oriented to it. A *transparent context* of reference/attribution is one in which a characterization of an object is given in terms of how an *observer* oriented to the object of his attention, quite *independently* of how the subject did. Quine remarks that opaque contexts of reference will not sustain substitutions of alternative descriptions of the object of orientation even when these alternative descriptions are correctly given for the same object. Thus, in the classic example, 'Oedipus' is the subject, his orientation is characterized as 'wanting to marry' and the object is 'Jocasta'. That it was true that 'Jocasta' was identical to, and could correctly be described as, 'Oedipus' mother', does *not* license a substitution of 'his mother' into the sentence: 'Oedipus wanted to marry Jocasta'. In transparent contexts of reference/attribution generally, such substitutions can readily be made. Thus, 'John kicked Fido' can transform to 'John kicked his dog' *iff* 'Fido' was 'John's dog'. It doesn't matter whether 'John' knew that, or even believed that, Fido was his dog: the substitution can go through here where it failed in the Oedipus example. Because we often encounter situations in which both observer-reporter and subject *share the same orientation to an object*, and would each give, or assent to, the same (perceptual) description(s) of it, the radical consequences of this distinction may be missed. Let me now put this distinction to work in terms of Fingarette's example above, and develop the argument.

In the account of M'Naghten's object of orientation, we have two alternatives. One is M'Naghten's own (or one to which he would have assented), namely, 'an act of desperate self-defense'. Call this account of the act 'opaquely attributive' – that is, 'true' for the subject, M'Naghten. The other is Fingarette's account, namely, 'assassination of the prime minister'. Call this account 'transparently attributive' – that is, true for the reporter independently of M'Naghten's orientation. To attempt a substitution here would be to generate a misleading – even a deceptive – report, for to predicate of M'Naghten an 'assassination' or 'assassination attempt' is to assign to him an action with its associated intention which he has implicitly (and explicitly, elsewhere) disavowed, just as predicating of Oedipus a desire to marry 'his mother' would be misleading, even though Jocasta was indeed Oedipus' mother.

In conceptualizing the activities and objects of the world, members may proffer accounts, reports, descriptions, etc. which, while in significant respects *true*, can none the less disguise their own perspectivality and mislead us into assuming that the *assessment of their truth*, or even its relevance, is shared where it may not be. Jayyusi gives an excellent example of this feature of account-construction at work, where the reporter's (possibly *true*) characterization of the religious affiliations of the contenders subtly implies that such a characterization was the relevant one held by the contenders:

'To drive the Christians out of their strongholds, the Moslems last week also imposed a tight *cordon sanitaire* around Christian areas' (*Time*, April 12, 1976). The implication is that the persons categorised (perhaps correctly) as 'Moslems' wanted to drive out persons whose relevant identity for the purposes at hand is 'Christian'. Strictly, it is not ever clear-cut, in such cases, whether the description is being offered in an opaque or transparent context – e.g., do the people involved in the offensive constitute the objects of their offensive as 'Christian' or is it the reporter who identifies them as being Christian and uses this characterisation? The implication of an opaque context is strong, however, precisely because of the co-selection of the category 'Moslem'.[37]

Where a range of other categories would have been true as well of those here categorized as 'Christian' (e.g. Lebanese, Phalangist, Arab, Maronite, fighter, gunmen, etc.), it is clear that the selection of a 'true characterization' does not in itself articulate the object(s) of orientation (perception, activity, etc.) beyond contention. *For the monitored coexistence of 'parallel' truths about phenomena may be subtly informative as to the basis of the particular 'true' designation of the perceived object, scene or setting.*

Let us here turn to more general concerns. In particular, it is time to characterize more fully what *sort* of investigations we have been outlining in the above discussions.

Grammars of Practical Cognition

'Grammar tells what kind of object anything is' (Wittgenstein).[38] If this is so, then it is clear that a study of 'grammar' would be a contribution to our understanding of what it is that enables us to know about the world, and, thus, would be a topic of inquiry into theoretical and practical cognition. The style of inquiry we have just been documenting may be called 'grammatical', but it is necessary to specify how this is so. Anscombe observes:

Plato saw the *grammatical* difference between 'Theaetetus' and 'walks', Wittgenstein, the *grammatical* difference between 'Theaetetus' and 'two'. If 'proper name' is a grammatical category, then so in his [Wittgenstein's] conception is 'numeral' and so is 'color-name' and so is 'psychological verb'. But by Wittgensteinian considerations even all of these turn out to be somewhat generic: that is, there are 'categorial' differences within each kind.'[39]

Grammars of concepts are rules which not only specify the linguistic frameworks within which words, phrases or types of words or phrases may be used, but also 'what counts as an application of' such expressions.[40] Grammars reveal the manifold connections between words and other words, phrases and expressions as these are used by 'masters of natural language', and the manifold connections between kinds of expression and the sorts of circumstance within which and about which they may be used. Since it is the use of words, phrases and other forms of expression which articulate our concepts, and it is our concepts which afford us knowledge of the world, however these may be ramified into accounts, hypotheses, theories or doctrinal systems, then the (evolving) grammar of our conceptual apparatus establishes (ongoingly) whatever intelligibility the world possesses for us. Exploring the connections and ramifications of concept-use for any domains of human interest within social contexts, practices and institutional arrangements – the grammars of cognition – becomes the overarching interest of the kind of 'epistemic' sociology I am concerned to exemplify here.

It might be argued that such inquiries are essentially 'non-empirical' in the sense that, although appeal is made to empirical (and even empirically reproduceable) instances of human activities (communications, action sequences, work routines) in documenting parameters of conceptual articulation and the ways in which 'phenomena' of various kinds are thus rendered intelligible, none the less the purpose of such analyses is 'logical' and thus ultimately distinct from a sociological enterprise. If, however, by 'logical' we mean 'grammatical' in Wittgenstein's (extended) sense (and many commentators prefer to speak of 'logical-grammatical' when interpreting Wittgenstein's thought), then it is clear that we can only arrive at our specifications of 'grammar' by inspecting actual occasions of reasoned use-and-context. We need for such a purpose elaborate 'reminders' when it is a question of examining facets of our commonplace cognition, and such 'reminders' take the form of systematically exemplifying 'data' derived from real-world social events and social processes. In the case of more esoteric or arcane pursuits, the requirement for actual instances or 'instantiations' is more obviously essential. Discussing *a priori* claims which emerge from empirical observations, Vendler remarks that 'almost any "game", or, in a larger context, almost any rule-governed activity, will be the source of such propositions. *And this domain may range so far as to include mathematics or the rules governing the synthesis of the manifold of experience.*'[41] In a similar vein, Kripke observes:

They [some philosophers] think that if something belongs to the realm of *a priori* knowledge, it couldn't possibly be known empirically. This is just a mistake. Something may belong in the realm of such statements that can be known *a priori* but may still be known by people on the basis of experience. To give a really common sense example: anyone who has worked with a computing machine knows that the computing machine may give an answer to whether such and such a number is prime. No one has calculated or proved that the number is prime. We, then, if we believe that the number is prime, believe it on the basis of our knowledge of the laws of physics, the construction of the machine, and so on. We therefore do not believe this on the basis of purely *a priori* evidence. We believe it (if anything is *a posteriori* at all) on the basis of *a posteriori* evidence . . . . So 'can be known *a priori*' doesn't mean 'must be known *a priori*'.[42]

I am not advancing the argument that *every* contribution to 'epistemic' sociology is of this kind, but those which may properly be called 'grammatical' inquiries are. This is one property of their analytical results which distinguishes them from more conventional ethnographies. It is my contention that such 'grammatical' inquiries extend the domain both of what used to be called 'ordinary-language philosophy'[43] and, perhaps more significantly for our purposes, the post-Schutzian sociology of knowledge.

Having mapped out a (small) portion of the background terrain, I shall turn now to a sustained discussion of the topic postponed until this point: the treatment to be accorded to the 'cognising subject' as a topic of analysis in epistemic sociology. The case to be made here is that the 'cognising subject' is not to be treated as a residual or essentially ineffable 'postulate' underlying the rest of epistemic analysis, constantly threatening to rise up and announce its independence from or its transcendence over the enterprise of socio-logical inquiry: rather, we need to subject the properties of such a 'subject' to grammatical analysis.

Notes

1 David Bloor, *Knowledge and Social Imagery* (Routledge & Kegan Paul, London, 1976).

2 See the contributions on this topic in Bryan R. Wilson (ed.), *Rationality* (Basil Blackwell, Oxford, 1974). See also the interesting exchange of views between Peter Winch and I.C. Jarvie on these issues in R. Borger and F. Cioffi (eds), *Explanation in the Behavioral Sciences* (Cambridge University Press, Cambridge, 1970).

3 See, *inter alia*, Nigel Harris's exemplary text, *Beliefs in Society: The Problem of Ideology* (C.A. Watts & Co., London, 1968); and Jurgen Habermas's influential *Legitimation Crisis* (Beacon Press, Boston, Mass., 1985).

4 See, for example, Thomas J. Scheff's *Being Mentally Ill: A Sociological Theory* (Weidenfeld & Nicolson, London, 1966), and his edited

collections, *Mental Illness and Social Processes* (Harper and Row, N.Y., 1967) and *Labeling Madness* (Spectrum, N.Y., 1975). A useful recent collection of papers in this tradition is David Ingleby (ed.), *Critical Psychiatry* (Penguin, London, 1980).

5   Cf. Wittgenstein, *Philosophical Investigations*, para. 88.

6   L. Wittgenstein, *On Certainty* eds G.E.M. Anscombe and G.H. von Wright, trans. D. Paul and G.E.M. Anscombe (Basil Blackwell, Oxford, 1969).

7   By 'praxiological' I shall mean: related to courses of practical human action, whether such action be primarily communicative or instrumental, interactional or object-involving.

8   Bloor, *Knowledge*, pp. 4–5.

9   See, e.g., L. Laudan, 'The Pseudo-Science of Science?', *Philosophy of the Social Sciences*, Vol. 11, No. 2, June 1981: Stephen P. Turner, 'Interpretive Charity, Durkheim and the "Strong Programme"', *Philosophy of the Social Sciences*, ibid.; and Warren Schmaus, 'Reasons, Causes and the "Strong Programme" in the Sociology of Knowledge', *Philosophy of the Social Sciences*, Vol. 15, No. 2, June 1985.

10 For materials relevant to such a general assessment from a point of view congenial to the arguments of the present work, see J. M. Atkinson, *Discovering Suicide* (University of Pittsburgh Press, 1979).

11 Bloor, *Knowledge*.

12 Wittgenstein, *On Certainty*, passages 160–1.

13 By 'logic' here, I do not mean to invoke the traditions of formal or symbolic logic as disciplinary enterprises, but rather to point to an analytic interest in specifying *forms of orderliness* in principled ways.

14 The classical 'problem of imputation' in the sociology of knowledge is articulated by Arthur Child in his papers: 'The Problem of Imputation in the Sociology of Knowledge', *Ethics*, Vol. 51, No. 2, 1941; and 'The Problem of Imputation Resolved', *Ethics*, Vol. 54, No. 1, 1944. Very few commentators agreed with Child that he had, in fact, settled the problem which he was instrumental in raising. For some useful discussion of this issue, see Barry Barnes, *Interests and the Growth of Knowledge* (Routledge & Kegan Paul, London, 1977), chapter 3.

15 Barnes, *Interests and the Growth of Knowledge*, p. 45.

16 W.W. Sharrock, 'On Owning Knowledge'. In Roy Turner (ed.), *Ethnomethodology* (Penguin, Harmondsworth, 1974).

17 Ibid., p. 49.

18 Lena Jayyusi, *Categorization and the Moral Order* (Routledge & Kegan Paul, London, 1984), pp. 52–6.

19 Ibid, p. 53.

20 Harvey Sacks, 'An Initial Investigation of the Usability of Conversational Data for Doing Sociology'. In David Sudnow (ed.), *Studies in*

Social Interaction; Sacks, 'On the Analyseability of Stories by Children'. In Turner (ed.), *Ethnomethodology*; Sacks, with Schegloff, 'Two Preferences for the Organisation of Reference to Persons and their Interaction'. In Psathas (ed.), *Everyday Language*; and Sacks, 'Hotrodder: A Revolutionary Category'. In Psathas, ibid. For an excellent review and development of 'categorization logic', see Jayyusi, *Categorization*.

21   Sacks, 'An Initial Investigation . . .'.

22   Ibid., p. 37.

23   H. Sacks, 'On the Analyseability of Stories by Children'. In Turner (ed.), *Ethnomethodology*, p. 225.

24   Ibid.

25   For some discussion of this example, taken from Terry Winograd, and related issues, see my 'Beliefs and Practical Understanding'. In Psathas (ed.), *Everyday Language*.

26   Some readers may note here my borrowing from J.J. Gibson the concept of an 'affordance' (J.J. Gibson, *The Ecological Approach to Visual Perception* (Lawrence Erlbaum, N.Y., 1986)). In Gibson's various writings on ecological optics and perceptual psychology, an 'affordance' of an object is its property of providing for some organism's activity toward or use of the object: thus, a large rock can 'afford' concealment, water can 'afford' drinking or swimming, etc. There is some similarity between this idea and G.H. Mead's concept of objects as 'telescoped acts'. In my usage, which is intendedly parasitic upon Gibson's, an 'affordance' of a 'use' of a category is what may be done with it inferentially by a recipient. It would not be helpful to speak only of the 'implications' of the use of a category in this context, since what may be inferred may not have been implied. On the basis of your telling me that you paid twice as much for your used car as its book value, I may warrantably infer that you were careless in checking its market value, but you may have sought to imply that, for you, money was no object. Conventionalizations which have engendered symmetries between specific sorts of implications and inferential options, such that it is usually reasonable to assume that what was implied is identical to what is inferred, should not blind us to the possibilities of disjunction. But disjunctions, too, should be examined for their possibly conventional rationalities.

27   Melvin Pollner, 'The Very Coinage of Your Brain: The Anatomy of Reality Disjunctures', *Philosophy of the Social Sciences*, Vol. 5, 1975.

28   Ibid., p. 426.

29   Cf. Gilbert Ryle's discussion of Zeno Vendler's *Res Cogitans* in his article, 'Mowgli in Babel', *Philosophy*, Vol. 49, No. 187, 1974.

30   Thomas S. Kuhn, *The Structure of Scientific Revolutions* (University of Chicago Press, Chicago, 1970), p. 111.

31   Ibid., p. 121.

32   Ullin T. Place, 'Some Remarks on the Social Relativity of Truth and the Analytic-Synthetic Distinction', forthcoming, p. 16. Emphasis added to final line.

33   Ibid., pp. 15–16.

34   Hanna F. Pitkin, *Wittgenstein and Justice* (California, University of California Press, 1972), pp. 111–12.

35   Herbert Fingarette, *The Meaning of Criminal Insanity* (University of California Press, 1972), p. 200.

36   W.V. Quine, *Word and Object* (Wiley, N.Y., 1960).

37   Jayyusi, *Categorization*, p. 157.

38   Wittgenstein, *Philosophical Investigations*, para. 373.

39   G.E.M. Anscombe, 'A Theory of Language?'. In Irving Block (ed.), *Perspectives on the Philosophy of Wittgenstein* (Basil Blackwell, Oxford, 1981), p. 156.

40   Cf. Stanley Cavell, 'The Claim to Rationality'. Unpublished doctoral dissertation, Harvard University, p. 131: cited in Pitkin, *Wittgenstein and Justice*, p. 118.

41   Zeno Vendler, 'Linguistics and the A Priori'. In Colin Lyas (ed.), Philosophy and Linguistics (Macmillan, N.Y., 1971), p. 256, emphasis added.

42   Saul Kripke, 'Naming and Necessity'. In D. Davidson and G. Harman (eds), *Semantics of Natural Language* (D. Reidel, Boston, 1972), p. 261.

43   Which was never really a 'philosophy' in the conventional sense, but began as an extension of logical analysis employed to undermine philosophical and quasi-scientific theses based upon deep (i.e. non-perspicuous) grammatical errors and developed into a distinctive mode of conceptual elucidation predicated upon hypothetical instances of discourse.

3

The Cognizing Subject

A good deal of modern sociological thinking has required of investigators that they make both explicit and implicit assumptions about the 'psychological properties' of human agents. Somewhat surprisingly, these conceptions have themselves been, in various respects, unsociological. I do not include here only the more obvious attempts to reduce sociological explanations to psychological ones, such as Homans' classic efforts,[1] nor the attempts to base sociological explanations upon abstract, generalized 'models of the actor' endowed with various motives, desires, needs or drives.[2] I have in mind, as well, the accounts of the nature of the 'self' and of 'mind' which are elaborated by, and which undergird the research of, symbolic-interactionist sociology.[3] These versions of the mental and/or cognitive characteristics of human agents have been widely influential in establishing a 'subjectivism in social science' to which, unfortunately, ethnomethodological work has incorrectly been assimilated by many.[4]

Mind, Self and Activity in Symbolic Interactionism

In his classic essay on 'the methodological position of symbolic interactionism', Blumer (who also coined the expression designating the school: symbolic interactionism) outlined its 'basic premises' as follows:

[H]uman group life consists of the fitting to each other of the lines of action of the participants; such aligning of actions takes place predominantly by the participants indicating to one another what to do and in turn interpreting such indications made by the others; out of such interaction people form the objects that constitute their worlds; people are prepared to act toward their objects on the basis of the meaning these objects have for them; human beings face their world as organisms with selves, thus allowing each to make indications to himself; human action is constructed by the actor on the basis of what he notes, interprets, and assesses; and the interlinking of such ongoing action constitutes organisations, institutions, and vast complexes of interdependent relations.[5]

Elaborating further on the theme of human actions as essentially based upon interpretation or symbolic self-indications of the meanings of actions, objects and situations, Blumer asserts that it was G.H. Mead who 'has sought to think through what the act of interpretation implies for the human being, human action, and human association.'[6] The 'key feature in Mead's analysis', according to Blumer, 'is that the human being has a self'.[7] By this, Mead is claimed to have meant that human beings can become the objects of their own actions. Referring to this property of humans as a 'mechanism', Blumer states that we are given a picture of 'the human being as an organism which confronts its world with a mechanism for making indications to itself. This is the mechanism that is involved in *interpreting* the actions of others. *To interpret the actions of another is to point out to oneself that the action has this or that meaning or character.*'[8] He continues:

Whatever the action in which he is engaged, the human individual proceeds by pointing out to himself the divergent things which have to be taken into account in the course of his action . . . . The process of constructing action through making indications to oneself cannot be swallowed up in any of the conventional psychological categories . . . . Self-indication is a moving communicative process . . . . The human being stands over against the world, or against 'alters', with such a process and not with a mere ego.[9]

Elsewhere, Blumer asserts that the 'self' is formed and realized through 'taking the roles of others with whom one is implicated in the joint activities of group life',[10] and that the 'process of *interpretation*' involved in interaction involves self-indications whose making 'is an *internalised* social process in that the actor is interacting with himself.'[11]

The view which emerges is significant for its extreme intellectualization of human activity in its insistence upon the ubiquitous relevance for actions of 'acts' or 'processes' of 'interpretation', comprising 'internalized' self-indications of 'meanings', enabled by a 'self' that is at once (somewhat contradictorily) both a 'mechanism' for making interpretations generally and a capacity whereby people can treat themselves as objects or topics of their own conduct. In his well-motivated effort to free the social sciences from over-simplifying and naive-positivistic versions of conduct which reduce it to sets of 'responses to stimuli', 'conditioned output', and the like, Blumer establishes a highly mentalistic conception of the human agent's capacities and conduct, notwithstanding his disavowal of 'ego' psychology and his view of social interaction as the primary subject-matter for sociological inquiry. The program sketched by Blumer was, of course, heeded more in principle than in research practice; after all, the complaint began, how can the investigator obtain reliable access to 'internalized' processes of interpretation or self-indication going on in people and supposedly necessary to our understanding of how their activities are produced and coordinated in the empirical world? How do we tell what 'meanings' people are subjectively indicating to themselves as a basis for their conduct? It seemed to many that only by a method of submersion within the social worlds inhabited by others could we even begin to achieve that form of 'participant observation' necessary to understanding what may be going on inside their minds. The investigator concerned to reveal the actors' 'interpretations' would have to become, for the period of his research inquiry at least, himself an enactor of the same roles taken over by the agents under study. The 'metaphysics' of this rationale for 'participant observation' was fundamentally a modern variant of the classic notion that one has to be Caesar to understand his conduct, or, at least, to *approximate* to such an understanding, since Caesar's (and anyone else's) interpretive operations are, by definition within this tradition, 'internal' acts or processes. Of course, much fine ethnographic work was developed by practitioners of 'participant observation' in sociology, and not all practitioners shared this metaphysical rationale for its methodological employment. None the less, this kind of thinking continued to nourish cognate conceptions of the role of 'subjectivity' in social-scientific theorizing. Manis and Meltzer, expounding upon symbolic interactionism's virtues in a well-known text in the field,[12] wrote of the requirement of 'feeling one's way inside the experience of the actor'[13] as a pre-requisite for the study of conduct: Brittan claims that, since 'the description and understanding of social conduct can only be mediated through some form of symbolic process which is located in consciousness', the greatest problem becomes 'the admitted difficulty of an adequate methodology to tease out the subtleties of consciousness',[14] and, further, that 'the inner world of intention, motive, attitude, etc., is the proper subject-matter of sociology – it constitutes the reservoir of social facts.'[15]

To paraphrase Wittgenstein, such a 'cloud of metaphysics' required to be swept away by 'a drop of grammar'. Such arguments as these were fundamentally the results of *conceptual* confusions. Commonplace, mutual understandings become elevated into 'interpretations', without regard for the occasionality of such a practice as 'interpreting' and its presuppositional requirements (such as the initial *in*comprehensible character of the to-be-'interpreted' action or communication, hardly a property of most everyday social activities). 'Self-indications' of 'meanings' which are taken to constitute *any* actions, objects and situations of agents turn out to be quite exceptional occurrences: we rarely need to reflect upon and give ourselves explanations of the meanings of what we or others around us are doing. Such undertakings require quite special sorts of context for their appropriateness and even their intelligibility. One does not need to resort to behavioristic reductionisms nor to an excessive appeal to the 'habits', 'unreflective routines' and 'spontaneities' of a good deal of human conduct to see that, taken seriously, such appeals to mentalistic acts of meaning-indications and interpretations 'in consciousness' are quite irrelevant to vast areas of human behavior. Further, the 'motives', 'intentions' and 'attitudes' supposedly inhabiting agents' 'inner worlds', and unavailable to any 'adequate methodology', are, in fact, mundanely and routinely avowed, ascribed and observably presupposed in practical social life. Of course, people can, and *sometimes* do, harbor 'undisclosed' assessments of things, generate 'private' interpretations of each others' actions, conceal their true intentions or motives from each other. These are not, however, methodological troubles for sociology, but member-assignable (and member-defeasible) accusations, excuses, claims and suspicions *within* their communicative affairs. Sociologists do not have to seek to transcend their membership limitations and become absolute *arbiters* of such accusations, suspicions, and so on. It is not the sociologist's function, *qua* sociologist, to go about claiming what someone's 'true' motives were if they are under practical contention, nor to propose that their subjects were entertaining 'undisclosed thoughts' of such-and-such a kind, nor to assert, unilaterally, how someone may privately have interpreted some ambiguous situation. This is *members'* practical business, for which they have occasioned, defeasible but public *criteria*.

Only on the assumption that sociologists must arrive at *incorrigible action-explanations* at the level of interactions could such conundrums stop them in their tracks. But if members themselves cannot have incorrigible versions of *all* of each others' conduct, why should anyone demand that of sociological inquirers into the logic of social affairs?

There is a significant sense in which the theoretical role assigned by much symbolic-interactionist thinking to the inner, the covert, the mental, the self and consciousness is a product of a complex of misleading and mistaken assumptions. One of these assumptions is that, since human behavior is not explainable mechanically on behavioristic principles then it *must* somehow be explainable 'mentally' on psychologistic principles. Another is the idea that, since people's actions, objects of orientation and situations of conduct do not literally come 'labelled' for what they are, somehow they must be 'labelled' anyway for their intelligibility to be vouchsafed, and since actual practices of 'labelling' are manifestly not an empirical feature of most scenes of orderly, rational social encounters the labelling (or 'interpreting' or 'conferral of meaning(s)') must, so the argument runs, be taking place 'internally', somewhere 'inside' the agents – usually 'in their minds'. A further feature of this collection of misconceptions is the notion that people's actual 'reasons' for their actions, as proffered and accepted or rejected in everyday life, are somehow *generically* defective as *explanations* for what they have done or are doing. While it is perfectly true that members sometimes give only 'rationalizations' and sometimes conceal their 'real' reasons for their conduct, it is equally true that they may give reason-explanations which truly explain their conduct. It requires special, situated *grounds for doubting* to entertain, rationally, the thought that a given reason might not be the 'real' reason for some action(s). Sociologists have no particular right or privilege, nor methodological necessity, to question members' reasons *in general.*

Indulging in the generic questioning of the validity of members' 'reasons' easily leads to a further fallacy, which is the theoretical imputation of the source of the 'real' reason to the mind of the agent, as if it could be discovered there if only sufficiently sophisticated techniques for accessing the 'inner' mental realm could be developed. Yet if agents are not guaranteed sovereignty as to what their avowed reasons for acting were or are, why should the putative contents of their *minds* be accorded any greater privilege in this regard? Even a 'reason' I may entertain in my undisclosed thoughts may, were it to be revealed, fail to pass muster as an acceptable, good enough or simply understandable explanation of what I did.

Meaning, Understanding and Interpretation

In addition to these considerations about action-explanation, lay or professional, there are issues raised concerning the possibility of 'understanding' what someone is doing. Dragons abound in this theoretical territory, all of which should be put to rest. A first issue, already touched on, is the propensity to substitute 'interpretation' for 'understanding' when depicting how members of a culture, lay and professional alike, deal with each others' communicative and other forms of conduct. Suffice to note that the attribution of 'interpreting' to people presupposes contexts of application by no means identical to those presupposed by the ascription of 'understanding'. For example, you remark to me that it is raining. I reply by saying that it had been predicted in yesterday evening's weather forecast. I understood what you said, just as you understood what you said, and we both understood my subsequent utterance. No issue of 'interpretation' arises here. But suppose I remark to you that it is raining, whereupon you become irritated and berate me by saying that the state of the weather is no excuse for not picking up the children from school. I reply that I had meant no such thing by my remark, that I was not proffering anticipatory excuses but simply making a casual observation about the weather. Someone listening may claim that you had 'misinterpreted the significance' of my remark, but could consistently propose that you had none the less 'understood' what I said. The examples could be ramified: not all conduct occasions or requires 'interpretation', and one can understand but misinterpret without contradiction. Moreover, by insisting upon the ubiquity of 'interpretation' in respect of conduct, symbolic interactionists are not only stretching the concept beyond its proper range of applications, but end up postulating interpretive activity as a continuously occurring 'mental' process. This may well be due to the common absence of contextually available criteria in people's conduct for the rational attribution of such activity to them, coupled to a stubborn adherence to the view that it *must* be going on all the same. If it isn't taking place in public, so to speak (as it could be discerned in the kind of communications or other conduct produced by one or more participant agents), then it is stipulated to occur 'in private', viz. mentally. But doesn't merely 'understanding' (an utterance, someone's action) involve 'grasping the meaning', and where is the meaning that is grasped? It isn't (usually) articulated in so many words, nor does it 'exist' in the object or situation understood in such and such a way. ('Did you understand what I said?' 'Yes! You want me to leave, right?' 'Fine, but where in my telling you to "get lost" was its meaning located?' A weird interchange!) Thus, we are led to believe, the 'meaning' is in the 'mind' of the one who understands.

Wittgenstein labored mightily to free us from the grip of this immensely tempting mentalistic version of 'understanding' (an utterance, an action, a situation, etc.). One of his major targets was the idea that understanding an utterance is a mental process or activity occurring contemporaneously with the experiential hearing of the physically articulated speaking. (This latter notion is still very much in vogue in cognitive theorizing today, although in this domain it has been relegated to the realm of the 'unconscious'.)[16] In combatting this pervasive misconception, Wittgenstein strives to expose its grip on us. He notes that: 'We don't get away from the idea that the sense of a sentence accompanies the sentence; is there with it',[17] and this, together with the view that 'understanding' has a present-continuous tense form characteristic of many genuine activity-or process-verbs such as 'running', 'hitting', 'spitting', 'speaking', 'writing', etc., nourishes the mentalistic version in which understanding is a mental *process* of grasping a 'sense' alongside the hearing (or reading) of a sentence. Further, we are tempted to think of the words and utterances which people speak as if they were in themselves mere 'sounds' or 'dead signs' which need life to be breathed into them by mental, 'meaning-endowing' operations. If we protest that we are not conscious of such operations as constituent features of our dealings with utterances, we may come to believe

that the difficulty of the task consists in our having to describe phenomena that are hard to get hold of, the present experience that slips quickly by, or something of the kind. Where we find ordinary language too crude, and it looks as if we were having to do, not with the phenomena of every-day, but with ones that 'easily elude us'.[18]

'The signs of our language seem dead without these mental processes,' Wittgenstein acknowledges. 'We are tempted to think that the action of language consists of two parts; an inorganic part, the handling of signs, and an organic part, which we may call understanding these signs, meaning them, interpreting them, thinking.'[19] All of this is exposed systematically as the mythology it is in Wittgenstein's painstaking treatment. There are several lines of attack. One is to undermine the notion that 'understanding' is a type of (fleeting) experience accompanying hearing, looking or reading: 'Someone tells me the route I have to take to some place and from there on. He asks "Did you understand?" I reply "Yes I did". – Do I mean to tell him what was going on within me during his explanation? – And after all that could be told him too.'[20] He urges us to try not to think of 'understanding' as any sort of 'mental process'. 'In the sense in which there are processes (including mental processes) which are characteristic of understanding, understanding is not a mental process.'[21] When someone suddenly understands (e.g. a principle for completing a number series), then perhaps he will have a special experience and even be able to describe it in some way, but what he describes is not his 'understanding': '. . . it is the *circumstances* under which he had such an experience that justify him in saying in such a case that he understands, that he knows how to go on.'[22] Although understanding is not itself merely a kind of 'behavior', it is manifested in behavior. Without such manifestation, there would be no way for the concept itself to be acquired and used properly, and no way in which to make a distinction between '*thinking that* one understands' and 'actually understanding':

Let us remember that there are certain criteria in a man's behavior for the fact that he does not understand a word; that it means nothing to him, that he can do nothing with it. And criteria for his 'thinking that he understands', attaching some meaning to the word, but not the right one. And, lastly, criteria for his understanding the word right.'[23]

Wittgenstein adds here that it is only the second of these three possibilities outlined which justify one in speaking sensibly of 'subjective understanding'.[24] If 'the grammar of the word "knows" is . . . closely related to that of "understands"',[25] then my saying: '(Now) I (suddenly) understand' is not to be describing a mental occurrence, but may be to declare myself as in possession of some knowledge. What distinguishes my actually understanding, i.e. having knowledge, from merely supposing or thinking that I do, from merely believing so, is nothing interior to my mind or brain (which I might find difficult to describe), but is my correct, ratifiable performance, my proper application, my exhibited capacity to do, say or in some other contextually appropriate manner to *satisfy the relevant criteria* for my having, indeed, actually understood whatever it was I *claimed* to have understood. Saying 'I understand' is not *eo ipso* to understand, and is not necessarily said *because* one really does understand: one can think that one understands and be shown to have been wrong. 'There are occasions when one rightly says "I understand, now I can go on", and then, when asked to go on (continue the series, whistle the theme, etc.), one suddenly finds one cannot. Does this inevitably mean that one was wrong in saying that one understood?' ask Baker and Hacker.[26] Their reply is illuminating here:

Clearly not – no more than when one says 'I can lift that heavy weight', and then bends down clumsily and slips a disc so that one cannot lift it. We make room for losing an ability between avowal and performance, and sometimes agree, *on the basis of further criteria*, that when a person said he could . . . he could, even though he was subsequently unable to.[27]

When Wittgenstein speaks of 'criteria' for understanding, he is not confining himself to the view that, since 'understanding' is not a mental process but akin to an ability, such 'criteria' are purely behavioral: 'The criteria which we accept for "fitting", "being able to", "understanding", are much more complicated than might appear at first sight. That is, the game with these words, their employment in the linguistic intercourse that is carried on by their means, is more involved – the role of these words in our language other – than we are tempted to think.'[28]

An explicit, first-person avowal of understanding is not a (quasi-) description of either a mental *or* a behavioral phenomenon, but a signal[29] which defeasibly betokens, in many cases, the possession of an ability or its sudden acquisition. But how can this be squared with 'understanding the *meaning* of an utterance or expression'? Doesn't that involve somehow getting behind the mere words or phrases used to their 'sense'? And isn't *that* something accomplished *mentally*? Wittgenstein remarks: 'But if you say: "How am I to know what he means, when I see nothing but the signs he gives?" then I say: "How is he to know what he means, when he has nothing but the signs either?" '[30] He continues: 'The absentminded man who at the order "Right turn!" turns left, and then, clutching his forehead, says "Oh! right turn" and does a right turn. – What has struck him? An interpretation?'[31] We are clearly meant here to reject the gratuitously over-intellectualized possibility which Wittgenstein presents. His (eventually) taking the right turn is, here, *sufficient* for us to say of the man that he 'grasped the meaning' of the instruction to 'turn right'. We do not have to suppose that he indulged in a silent soliloquy in which he explained to himself the 'meaning' of the expression before he could follow the instruction articulated in it. And if a 'meaning' is not *embedded in an explanation* of a meaning, whether spoken or 'thought up', where could it be found? If one is here tempted to say: in his 'unconscious mind', then it remains to be clarified how an explanation of the meaning of an expression *of which one is wholly unaware* can inform one of its sense!

Baker and Hacker elsewhere pick up this favored cognitivist theme and subject it to Wittgensteinian-inspired grammatical criticism. According to many theoreticians in cognitive science, psycholinguistics and other fields of psychologistic endeavor, it is argued that 'understanding (an utterance)' is or involves a process of computation in which one begins with 'sounds' as 'inputs', applies rules of syntax and semantics on the analogy of a computer operating according to its program, and 'derives' the 'meaning' of what has been heard (provided that the computation was correctly, albeit mechanically, undertaken).[32] Baker and Hacker argue as follows:

Just how misguided this picture is becomes evident if, bearing in mind that understanding is not an act, activity or state, we view the matter from the perspective of a normal speaker who understands the sentences he himself utters and knows what he is saying by using them. . . . when does a speaker understand a sentence he utters [according to the computationalist account]? *Before* he utters it? But how is it possible for him to understand what he says before he says it? Indeed, what *is* there to understand before the sentence is spoken? Is it that he speaks it to himself quickly before he speaks it aloud? But that idea merely generates an infinite regress, for the question of when he understands the sentence he quietly says to himself now arises. If only *after* he says it to himself, does he then say it to himself without understanding it, as it were, to see what sense it will make? This is absurd. But if *before* he says it to himself, then how is *that* possible? . . . Does it then follow that a speaker does *not* understand what he says aloud until after he has said it, that he must wait to hear what he says before he can know what it means? This too is absurd.[33]

The solution to these conundrums, which are an artifact of construing 'understanding' as an inner process of meaning-computation operating upon mere 'sounds' (or 'dead signs'), is to deny that a speaker's understanding what he says is *any* kind of occurrence at all, 'any more than being able to play chess occurs before or after moving a chess piece in a game'.[34] We must also deny that an 'utterance', just because it has acoustic properties, is experienced as merely a 'string of *sounds*'.

'Subjective Sovereignty' and 'Private Language'

Wittgenstein's refutation of the idea of 'understanding' (what someone says, what someone is doing) as a mental act or process which accompanies hearing what is said (or seeing what is done) may now be connected to his critical onslaught against Cartesian (mis)conceptions of 'mental' and 'experiential' language-use more generally. According to (the assumptions of) this tradition, each of us can only know the meaning of a 'mental' term in virtue of what it refers to within our own immediate or direct sphere of experience. One standard precept would be, for example, that it is only by effecting an 'internal cognition' or an internal identification of a mental or experiential 'existent' that one can ascertain the meaning of a word used to 'designate' it. Each of us can only know from his or her *own* case what any given mental or experiential concept means, and thus it is possible that we may each 'mean' different things by our use of the mental vocabulary. Our 'language' for the mental and experiential domains is, thus, private. A central argument advanced against this conception is that for anything to count as a 'language', it must comprise a range of signs or symbols which are used 'according to rules'. We can understand language because we are *socialized* into 'grasping its rules'. However, can't *any* rule be variously interpreted? Can't there be purely private cases of rule-interpretations and rule-followings?

> . . . there is a way of grasping a rule which is *not* an *interpretation*, but which is exhibited in what we call 'obeying the rule' and 'going against it' in actual cases.
>
> Hence there is an inclination to say: every action according to the rule is an interpretation. But we ought to restrict the term 'interpretation' to the substitution of one expression of the rule for another.
>
> And hence also 'obeying a rule' is a practice. And to *think* one is obeying a rule is not to obey a rule. Hence it is not possible to obey a rule 'privately': otherwise thinking one was obeying the rule would be the same thing as obeying it.[35]

In these passages, Wittgenstein notes that rule-following, doing something in accord with a rule, are *practices* which people have learned how to engage in through their socialization. Although one way of showing that one has mastered a rule can consist in providing an acceptable, purpose-relevant, contextually appropriate 'interpretation' of it (e.g. as when one remarks that the rule against parking in a given space may be interpreted as not applying to ambulances picking up injured people), there are many other ways of showing that one has mastered a given rule, including the ways in which one actually behaves in some circumstances where such a rule is relevantly applicable even though one may not be able to come up with a discursive 'interpretation' of it. Moreover, any rule can make sense, be applied or followed, *only* against the general background of socially shared institutions, practices and techniques of conduct which furnish criteria for distinguishing instances of actual rule-following from those in which agents may *profess to be* following some rule but cannot be found to be doing so, where they may *think* that they are, but in fact are not. There is, in other words, no such thing (logically) as 'solitary, private rule-following *ab initio*' for language-use nor for any other human activity. Colin McGinn, however, argues that this 'social' conception of rule-following is mistaken. He doubts 'whether the very *notion* of grasping a rule requires sometime membership in a community of rule-followers.[36] He sees no contradiction in the supposition that a god might have 'created a single rule-follower alone in the universe for all time'.[37] Perhaps so, but only by having endowed this solitary rule-follower with the kind of discriminatory, conceptual and behavioral resources which the rest of us mere mortals acquire from our socialization in communication communities. 'Rules' are acquired and embedded in explanations of rules, in instructions in their use, in adducing examples of their correct application, in correcting neophyte mistakes in their use, in training, checking and the kindred practices of a community within which there is already sufficient consensus as to what could *count as* 'obeying a rule', 'following a rule' or 'acting in accordance with a rule' as *distinct from* merely 'claiming (incorrectly, mistakenly) to have followed a rule', 'seeming to have followed a rule', or 'thinking that one is following a rule'.

The word 'agreement' and the word 'rule' are *related* to one another, they are cousins . . .
    'So you are saying that human agreement decides what is true and what is false?' – It is what human beings *say* that is true and false; and they agree in the *language* they use. That is not agreement in opinions but in form of life.[38]

Rule-formulation, rule-explanation, rule-use, rule-following, rule-application, rule-teaching, 'introducing a rule', 'appealing to rules', 'changing the rules', 'bending the rules' and a host of related practices presuppose (the possibility, attainability of) social agreements in judgments, in practices, in *action*.

Not only rules, but also examples are needed for establishing a practice. Our rules leave loop-holes open, and the practice has to speak for itself. We do not learn the practice of making empirical judgments by learning rules: we are taught *judgments* and their connexion with other judgments. A *totality* of judgments is made plausible to us.[39]

A key point in all of this is *not* simply to argue that an always isolated or eternally solitary being could not follow a rule because his individual memory might fail him in making future applications of it, unbeknownst to him, and no other person could detect the mistake and correct it, thus depriving him of the sovereign right to assert that he was 'following' – as distinct from merely '*thinking that* he was following' – a rule. The 'community-conception' of what rule-following requires is somewhat different: it proposes that, in the absence of *any* form of *social* or *trans*personal agreement whatsoever as to criteria for 'following a rule', we would not be able to ratify an avowal of nor to ascribe *either* 'rule-following' behavior *or* 'mistaken attempt(s) at rule-following'. In just the same sense, Wittgenstein argues that, without background agreement about what constitutes 'calculating', in *no* given instance could one attribute either 'calculating correctly' to someone *or* 'calculating *in*correctly' as well! The forging of new criteria, or a new background consensus, in respect of a 'practice' is required for the concept of that practice even to make *sense*, let alone for it to be seen and judged as correctly or incorrectly, appropriately or inappropriately, carried out. As we proposed earlier, intelligibility is intersubjective.

The domain for which assertions about 'private language' and 'subjective sovereignty' are most commonly proposed is, of course, that of our 'mental, 'experiential' or 'inner' realm. Wittgtenstein reminds us that any 'inner process' stands in need of 'outward criteria'.[40] If we *do* have a concept of any 'subjective' or 'inner process' (e.g. calculating in the head, dreaming, conjuring up a mental image, engaging in silent soliloquy), there must be *inter*subjective criteria for the justification of their ratified avowal and ascription. 'For if I need a justification for using a word, it must also be one for someone else.'[41] A claimed 'justification' which *could* not, in principle, be *counted as such* by *anyone* else, is no *justification* at all. Without even the *possibility* of an intersubjectively ratifiable justification, or the possibility of satisfying public criteria for mental or experiential claims, no *concepts* for such mental or experiential claims are themselves possible. Although a pre-linguistic infant can *have* a 'pain', it cannot be said to '*know that it has* a pain', nor to '*know* that it is in pain': knowledge-claims of this type are not possible from the child nor on its behalf prior to its acquisition of the concept of 'pain'. For it cannot satisfy the criteria for such a 'knowledge'-ascription. However, criterial satisfaction sufficient for ratification by others in the case of first-person experiential or mental avowals (such as 'I'm in pain!', 'I had a dream last night', 'I had this vivid image of her', etc.) need not consist in evidence that people have *used* criteria in *coming up with* their claims. 'What I do is not, of course, to identify my sensation by criteria: but to repeat an expression. But this is not the *end* of the language-game: it is the beginning.'[42] I do not 'identify' a sensation, the having had a dream, the mental image, by *employing* criteria, but my avowals of such things, or the non-linguistic conduct I exhibit which *shows* such things (e.g. that I am pain) must *satisfy* (intersubjective) criteria. It is only because, for example, I have exhibited a public reaction to a pain I have that I give others a basis for training me in the language for sensations: my satisfying a public criterion for 'being in pain' is what enables others to teach me the 'concept' of pain. My reactions, my narratives, my conduct more generally, its context, the objects of my avowals (where *intentional* mental phenomena are concerned, e.g. images *of*, recollections *of*, thoughts *about*, dreams *of*, etc.), their circumstances of avowal, the form or 'design' of my avowal, the entire relevant segment of a 'weave of (social) life' is criterially implicated in any act of (implicitly or explicitly) *ratifying* a first-person 'psychological' claim or avowal. This holds also for *defeating* an avowal; determining its incoherence, its impossibility, its implausibility, its evidencing 'confusion', 'hallucination', 'delusion', 'irrationality' and so on.

In a very important passage in *Zettel*, Wittgenstein considers what is involved in giving a description of human behavior. He says: 'How could human behavior be described? Surely only by sketching the actions of a variety of humans, as they are all mixed up together. What determines our judgment, our concepts and reactions, is not what *one* man is doing *now*, an individual action, but the whole hurly-burly of human actions, *the background against which we see any action*.'[43] There could be no clearer statement of the thesis of the *social* constitution of individual 'mind' and 'conduct' than that.

The Human Agent as Unconscious 'Information-Processor'

If culture furnishes the rules and criteria for the interactive (and, derivatively, for the solitary) conceptualization of the mental, there still remains the cognitive-psychological claim for a distinctively supraphysiological level of an unconscious mind. This model replaces the Freudian account, in which the unconscious mind was thought of according to hydraulic-flow metaphors, with a 'computationalist' conception, in which the 'unconscious mind' engages in the 'processing and transformation of information'[44] received through the sensory organs of the body. Indeed, this information-processing account has led to a completely novel form of 'private-language' argument, one in which the 'language' in question is not the postulated 'private language' of mind and experience criticized by Wittgenstein, but a 'language' within which 'information' is processed, stored and transformed in the central nervous system: the 'language of the brain' or 'the language of thought' is the hypothesized neurophysiological equivalent to a computer's internal machine code.

This theoretical construction has an interesting genealogy. It is instructive to note that Turing, who originated the mathematical idea of 'machine computability',[45] and Shannon, who originated the communications-theoretic concept of 'information',[46] both established the general notion of a *bit* (a binary digit) as a precisely measurable unit of an 'amount of information', and both claimed for their respective theoretical work relevance for psychology and neurophysiology, among other sciences. It is useful to explore some of their basic ideas a little further before discussing some of the cognitivist claims based upon their use.

It is possible to 'encode' any decimal number in a binary system consisting exclusively of 0 and 1. The *decimal system* of representation uses base 10 and ten numerals (0, 1, 2, 3, . . . 9) to express any arbitrary number, where to write numbers larger than 9 we assign meaning to the *position* of a numeral within an array: thus, 664 equals (6 times 10 squared) plus (6 times 10 to the power 1) plus (4 times 10 to the power 0). The digit which is furthest to the right (in this example, 4) is the coefficient of the zero-th power, the next digit is the coefficient of the first power, the next is the coefficient of the second power, and one can continue leftwards. By contrast, in a *binary system* of representation, the base is 2, and only the two numerals 0 and 1 are required to express a number. Thus, the decimal number 19 may be written as: 10011. This is because 19 equals (*1* times 2 to the power 4) plus (*0* times 2 to the power 3) plus (*0* times 2 to the power 2) plus (*1* times 2 to the power 1) plus (*1* times 2 to the power 0).

A group of bits [1s or 0s] having a significance is a *bite, word* or *code*. For example, to represent the 10 numerals (0, 1, 2, 3, . . . 9) and the 26 letters of the English alphabet would require 36 different combinations of 1's and

0's ... a minimum of 6 bits per bite are required to accommodate all the alphanumeric characters ... a bite is sometimes referred to as a *character*.[47]

In digital computing machines, a number can be represented in serial form by a train of pulses. A 1 is implemented by an electronic pulse, and a 0 by no pulse, usually synchronized to a master clock-pulse.

The pulses (or absence of pulses) occur serially, one after another, and the information (number, instruction) conveyed by this pulse sequence may be transmitted from one place to another over a single communication link (i.e., in the simplest case, a pair of wires). This mode of representing information is described by the word *serial*. Alternatively, we may devise that each of the pulses (or absence of pulses) needed to represent the information occurs simultaneously on a separate channel .... This mode of operation is described by the word *parallel*.[48]

If pulse trains are transmitted along wiring circuits in a 'logic system' comprising an array of switching gates called AND-gates, OR-gates, NOT-gates and FLIP-FLOPS, various functions can be implemented in the hardware of the computer, and 'information' can be 'stored'. Thus, for example, a NOT-gate has a single input and a single output and performs the operation of NEGATION in accordance with the following principle: the output of the circuit takes on the 1 state if and only if the input does NOT take on the 1 state. Since it inverts the 'sense' of the output with respect to the input, it is also known as an 'inverter'. A FLIP-FLOP circuit consists of two interconnected NOT circuits. Because of this particular interconnection, the circuit may persist indefinitely in a state in which one part is ON while the other is OFF, or vice-versa. 'Since the FLIP-FLOP has two stable states it may be used to *store* one bit of information.'[49] For this reason, a FLIP-FLOP circuit is also referred to as a 'binary'.

In the design of a computer, then, there are realized the concepts of binary-digital representation or 'bits', electronic correspondences to such digital representations (1 for ON, 0 for OFF), alphanumeric encoding in 'bits', the possibility of encoding any information expressible alphanumerically, the transformation of such encoded information into electronic pulse trains, the possibility of effecting transformations of such pulse trains via hard-wired circuitry to implement 'computations', and the possibility of 'storing' information thus encoded in circuitry.

Although some of the details may vary, it was none the less both Shannon's and Turing's idea that, since nerves (such as neurones) in human beings (as in other organisms) operate in a binary fashion, either firing (ON) or not-firing (OFF) and are arranged in complex interconnections (via synapses and dendrites, etc.), and since it has been shown possible to represent any alphanumerically-expressible information in binary-digital form, perhaps the brain works analogously to an electronic digital information-processor. Psychologists such as Miller[50] and philosophers such as Putnam[51] soon began to extol the virtues of such a 'model' of CNS information-processing, and Simon's work[52] and his collaboration with Newell[53] began to generate the concept of the human nervous system as an unconscious 'physical-symbol manipulation' system by analogy to the operation of a computer. Such a picture forms a central component of the theoretical imagery of cognitive science, that branch of cognitive studies which is nourished by developments in the field of artificial intelligence (AI) computer programming and technology.

This model soon faced important detractors, however. Putnam, for example, originally most sympathetic to it, now declares that '[T]he Turing machine model need not be taken seriously as a model of the functional organisation of the brain. Of course, the brain has digital elements – the yes-no firing of the neurons – but whether the larger organisation is correctly represented by something like a flow-chart for an algorithm or by something quite different we have no way of knowing right now.'[54] G.P. Moore also reminds us that 'Much that has been said on the subject of information processing by the nervous system is either misinformed, incorrect or only metaphorical. The simple statement "neurons process information" poses profound philosophical problems and consists of three words whose meaning is unclear – in contrast, say, with the statement "neurons transmit impulses", which has an unambiguous meaning under properly defined circumstances.'[55]

Skepticism about the nature of brain impulses and their possible functions in digitalizing 'information' (whether serial or parallel 'processing' is involved) is, in itself, insufficient to undermine the power of the computational metaphor in cognitive studies. None the less, such comments as these should alert us to the fact that models of 'cognitive information processing' are not based upon 'discoveries' in neurophysiology; rather, they arise from attempts to pursue the empirical and theoretical implications of *postulating* a commonality between *any* type of entity which can, in some sense, be said to 'process information'. And there is surely a vernacular sense in which people do exactly this: they produce and understand oral and written communications; they weigh alternatives and solve problems; they recall things; they engage in reasoning, inference, calculation and decision-making, and in sundry other ways generate, handle, transmit and transform 'information'. It should be noted, though, that it is *people* who do these things, *not* their brains, even though their brains enable them to do what they do. Ordinarily, such 'information' as people are engaged in receiving and 'processing' exists in discursively available formats. One cannot derive information in this sense *simply* by seeing and hearing (i.e. by registering 'input'): after all, one can see without recognizing, hear without listening, look without knowing what one is looking at, hear without understanding, etc. Thus, to glean information from the exercise of the sensory modalities in the full-fledged discursive sense of 'information' (as distinct from both 'misinformation' and elementary 'stimulation') – e.g. to derive *knowledge* that X is the case – itself presupposes a background of conceptualization. Wittgenstein addresses an aspect of this issue in the course of his discussion of the limits of 'ostensive definition' (i.e. definition of something by pointing at it as one introduces the concept for it) as a part of learning a first natural language:

Now one can ostensively define a proper name, the name of a color, the name of a material, a numeral, the name of a point of the compass and so on. The definition of the number two, 'That is called "two"' – pointing to two nuts – is perfectly exact. – But how can two be defined like that? The person one gives the definition to doesn't know what one wants to call 'two'; he will suppose that 'two' is the name given to *this* group of nuts! – He *may* suppose this; but perhaps he does not. He might make the opposite mistake; when I want to assign a name to this group of nuts, he might understand it as a numeral. And he might equally well take the name of a person, of which I give an ostensive definition, as that of a color, of a race, or even of a point of the compass. That is to say: an ostensive definition can be variously interpreted in *every* case.

Perhaps you say: two can only be ostensively defined in *this* way: 'This number is called "two"' . . . . But this means that the word 'number' must be explained before the ostensive definition can be understood . . .

So one might say: the ostensive definition explains the use – the meaning – of the word when the overall role of the word in language is clear.[56]

Suppose, however, that training in a variety of language-games in which such concepts have a role inculcates in the learner a practical mastery of the use of the concepts in question. Does this entail that they have 'stored' conceptual 'information' which can subsequently be used in gleaning (and storing) additional 'information' from the exercise of their senses? We do attain 'knowledge of' the world, and much of it is in (acquired and deployed in) propositional or discursive form; it is 'knowledge that' such-and-such obtains, 'knowledge of', 'knowledge about', such-and-such. (Recall that much of our knowledge in this domain is knowing-*how*, a matter of the acquisition of *abilities* rather than propositions.) Where do we 'keep' such knowledge when we are not 'using' it? We speak of 'background knowledge': where is it 'stored'? 'In the brain or central nervous system' is a common 'answer' to such general questions as these, and the information-processing and storage models based upon Shannon's and Turing's original conceptual schemes appear well suited to making such an answer scientifically respectable. Prior to the development of concepts such as 'binary digitization' of 'information', 'bits', 'encoding information', 'representation in a bite', etc., ideas about brains' storing knowledge appeared metaphysical at best. Now, it seems, they can be given a precise meaning, and one which accords well, at least on the surface, with what is known about the workings of neuron-cells and their electrical firing patterns and their 'wiring' or interconnections.

All of this assumes that discursively represented information may be decomposed into 'units' which are binary-encodable. One orthodoxy here has been to conceive of the elementary alphanumeric possibilities available in a natural language as the 'units'; thus, for English, it takes 36 different combinations of 1s and 0s to represent the alphabet of 26 letters and the decimal system of number-representation. Other systems may be devised for use in computational machinery. For example, the IBM convention established eight bits representing a character (of a 256-character alphabet) as one bite or *byte*. But how could one ascertain the 'system' putatively 'used' by the human brain? Just because any 'message' can be converted into n binary digits does not mean that it contains n 'units of information' in a larger sense. It would be clearly absurd to claim that because a message could be written with twelve letters, it therefore consisted in twelve 'units of information' in some context-independent fashion.

It is even more difficult to see how our ordinary concept of 'information' (as 'knowledge-that') could be readily mapped onto Shannon's scheme for measuring 'amounts of information' in formal communication theory. In Shannon's scheme, an amount of information is particularized to specifications, in terms of binary digits or 'bits', of binary decisions contributing to the elimination of possibilities represented by the occurrence of some event or state of affairs. Thus, a general formula can be expressed for computing the amount of information generated by the reduction of n possibilities (all equally likely) to 1. In Dretske's concise summary: 'If s (the *source*) is some mechanism or process the result of which is the reduction of n equally likely possibilities to 1, and we write $I(s)$ to denote the amount of information associated with, or generated by, s, then: $I(s) = \log n$, where log is the logarithm to base 2.'[57] Clearly, this is a highly restricted sense of 'amount of information' and it belongs to very specific contexts of application, within which it functions most usefully. Although both Shannon and Turing developed the concept of a 'bit' of information from the Boolean algebra in formal logic, their deployment of the concept is quite different in important respects. Let us return to the example of an elementary digital computer operating upon bits and bit-strings.

As we saw earlier, the binary representation for the decimal number 19 is: 10011. Suppose that such a string were converted into a system of pulses: ON – OFF – OFF – ON – ON (or, in a 'double-rail' dynamic logic system, a pulse on one lead indicates that the variable has the 0 value whereas a pulse on the other lead signifies a 1). Now suppose that a train of neural impulses were to be discovered (discretely) operating in a manner isomorphic with the pulse train just described. Would that indicate to us that the neurons were generating a binary representation for the decimal number 19? According to what criteria? Under what circumstances? It is as well to bear in mind Heil's point that:

the sense in which we might want to say that the internal 'machine language' of a digital computer is symbolic – the sense, that is, in which it could be said to have meaning – is parasitic on its relation to a suitable programming language, and the sense of this language, in turn, dependent on its application by a suitable, language-using programmer. The programmer provides an *essential* link between states of the machine and states of affairs in the world to which the former 'refer'.[58]

In this, Heil's 'programmer' is the computer technician who has devised the procedures for translating a higher-level programming language into assembly language and ultimately into the appropriate machine code.[59] The dangers of a 'projection error' loom large – that is, the attribution of a code and a set of operations *in accord with* the input and output of some entity to the inner operations of the entity itself. Within the realm of Cognitive Science, a logical system which may be used to *describe*, for example, an arithmetical calculation or the syntactical assembly of a well-formed, grammatical sentence in a natural language, is too readily ascribed to the producer of that calculation or sentence *as a feature of its actual production*. It is this which results in so much of the 'pan-logicism' of neo-Cartesian, information-processing models of minds/brains.

If there are no general 'translation' rules for converting person-level information (the myriad of kinds of discursive knowledge we acquire and use) into sub-personal 'information' (in the sense of the communications engineer or computer technician), supposedly 'processed by' the central nervous system, then cognitivist accounts of human conduct which are based upon postulating 'information-processing' models remain at best unmotivated and, at worst, empty.

If the foregoing arguments are sound, then they may serve as critical foundations for establishing a radically 'sociologizing' attitude to the relationship between the individual and society, between 'mind' and 'culture' and between the 'contents of consciousness' and the sociocultural matrix. This attitude is not nourished by the formulation and 'testing' of causal models of human conduct, knowledge or belief. It is not served by proposing either 'external' or 'internal' explanations for such phenomena. Rather, it is best advanced when we pause to reflect in some detail on the manifold ways in which we are, in every dimension of our being, from our initial appearance as infant organisms to our full-fledged status as 'free agents' and 'responsible adults', constituted and reconstituted by the sociocultural and social-interactional resources of the species in general and of the co-inhabitants of our local social environments in particular.

Notes

1 George Homans, 'Bringing Men Back In', *American Sociological Review*, Vol. 29, December 1964; 'The Sociological Relevance of Behaviorism'. In R.L. Burgess and D. Bushell Jr (eds), *Behavioral Sociology* (Columbia University Press, N.Y., 1969); and his *Social Behavior: Its Elementary Forms* (Harcourt, N.Y., 1974, revised edition).

2 Cf. Dennis Wrong, 'The Over-socialized Conception of Man in Modern Sociology', *American Sociological Review*, Vol. 26, April 1961, and widely reprinted.

3 For a useful overview of this field, see Paul Rock, *The Making of Symbolic Interactionism* (Rowman & Littlefield, N.J., 1979).

4 E.g. David Rubinstein, 'Subjectivism in Social Science'. In his *Marx and Wittgenstein* (Routledge & Kegan Paul, London, 1981), and the now standard resource for this mistaken characterization: Lewis A. Coser, 'Two Methods in Search of a Substance', *American Sociological Review*, Vol. 40, December 1975.

5 Herbert Blumer, 'The Methodological Position of Symbolic Interactionism'. In his *Symbolic Interactionism: Perspective and Method* (Prentice-Hall, N.J., 1969), p. 49.

6 Blumer, 'Society as Symbolic Interaction'. In ibid., p. 79.

7 Ibid.

8 Ibid., p. 80, emphasis added.

9 Ibid., p. 81.

10 H. Blumer, 'The Methodological Position.. ', op. cit., p. 21n.

11 Ibid., p. 5. Italics added.

12 J.G. Manis and B.N. Meltzer (eds), *Symbolic Interaction* (Allyn & Bacon, Boston, 1967. Revised in 1974 and 1978).

13 Ibid., p. 1.

14 Arthur Brittan, *Meanings and Situations* (Routledge & Kegan Paul, London, 1973), p. 11.

15 Ibid., p. 25.

16 For some discussion of this theoretical claim in cognitive science, see J. Coulter, 'On Comprehension and "Mental Representation"' in G.N. Gilbert and C.C. Heath (eds), *Social Action and Artificial Intelligence* (Gower Press, Nottingham, 1984).

17 L. Wittgenstein, *Zettel*, ed. Anscombe & von Wright, trans. Anscombe (Basil Blackwell, Oxford, 1967), para. 139.

18 Wittgenstein, *Philosophical Investigations* (PI), para. 436.

19 L. Wittgenstein, *The Blue and Brown Books* (Basil Blackwell, Oxford, 1958), p. 3.

20 Wittgenstein, *Zettel*, para. 193.

21 Wittgenstein, *PI*, para. 154.

22 Ibid., para. 155.

23 Ibid., para. 269.

24 Ibid.

25 Ibid., para. 150.

26 G.P. Baker and P.M.S. Hacker, *Wittgenstein: Understanding and Meaning* (Basil Blackwell, Oxford, 1980), p. 607.

27 Ibid., emphasis added.

28 Wittgenstein, *PI*, para. 182.

29 Ibid., para. 180.

30 Ibid., para. 504.

31 Ibid., para. 506.

32 See, *inter alia*, Jerry A. Fodor, *The Language of Thought* (Thomas Crowell, N.Y., 1975); for some discussion, see J. Coulter, *Rethinking Cognitive Theory* (Macmillan, London, 1983).

33 G.P. Baker and P.M.S. Hacker, *Language, Sense and Nonsense* (Basil Blackwell, Oxford, 1984), p. 349.

34 Ibid.

35 Wittgenstein, *PI*, paras 201–2.

36 Colin McGinn, *Wittgenstein on Meaning* (Basil Blackwell, Oxford, 1984), p. 196ff. Cf. S. Blackburn, 'The Individual Strikes Back', *Synthese*, Vol. 58, 1984. Blackburn claims that a central Wittgensteinian argument against 'private language' (distinguishing *being* correct from thinking that one is correct in a use of a rule, where the possibility of making such a distinction derives from criteria grounded in systems of social practice) could be extended to generate a 'skepticism' about the 'authority' of such practices themselves. According to this view, a community as a whole might be mistaken in its claims to follow its own rules correctly. This argument misses the point of Wittgenstein's appeal here to public and social practices, socialization, training and intersubjective justification. He did not claim that any *given* community *must* always be considered rational (thus ruling out of court by pure stipulation the logical possibility of collective insanity, etc.); rather, the argument is that any judgement about people's rule-following conduct (or lack of it), in the singular *or* the plural cases, requires criteria for rational justification. A determination that *some* particular collectivity or 'community' is mad or is engaged in a conspiracy to deceive presupposes the existence of publicly enforceable criteria. A generic scepticism about *every* collectivity, however, removes the very grounds required for making *any* such determination. Wittgenstein remarks: 'Following a rule is analogous to obeying an order . . . . But what if one person reacts in one way and another in another to the order and the training? Which one is right? Suppose you came as an explorer into an unknown

country with a language quite strange to you. In what circumstances would you say that the people there gave orders, understood them, obeyed them, rebelled against them, and so on? *The common behavior of mankind is the system of reference by means of which we interpret an unknown language.*' (PI, para. 206; emphasis added)

37 Ibid., p. 198.
38 Wittgenstein, *PI*, paras. 224, 241.
39 Wittgenstein, *On Certainty*, paras 139–40.
40 Wittgenstein, *PI*, para. 580.
41 Ibid., para. 378.
42 Ibid., para. 290.
43 Wittgenstein, *Zettel*, para. 567, final emphasis added.
44 Among many useful sources for this by now standard view of mind in cognitive studies, see Owen Flanagan Jr, *The Science of the Mind* (MIT Press, Cambridge, Mass., 1984).
45 See Andrew Hodges, *Alan Turing: The Enigma* (Burnett Books, London, 1983).
46 See Claude Shannon and Warren Weaver, *The Mathematical Theory of Communication* (University of Illinois Press, Urbana, 1963); and, for an excellent account of the fundamental postulates of his theoretical system, Fred I. Dretske, *Knowledge and the Flow of Information* (MIT Press: Bradford Books, Cambridge, Mass., 1981), chapters 1, 2.
47 Jacob Millman and Herbert Taub, 'Logic Circuits'. In their *Pulse, Digital and Switching Waveforms* (McGraw-Hill, N.Y., 1965), p. 309.
48 Ibid., p. 311.
49 Ibid., p. 343.
50 George A. Miller, 'What is Information Measurement?', *The American Psychologist*, Vol. 8, January 1953.
51 Hilary Putnam, 'Minds and Machines'. In Sidney Hook (ed.), *Dimensions of Mind* (Collier-Macmillan, London, 1960).
52 Herbert A. Simon, *The Sciences of the Artificial* (MIT Press, Cambridge, Mass., 1969).
53 Alan Newell and H.A. Simon, *Human Problem Solving* (Prentice-Hall, N.J., 1972).
54 Hilary Putnam, 'Reductionism and the Nature of Psychology'. In John Haugeland (ed.), *Mind Design* (Bradford Books, Vermont, 1981), p. 216. Interestingly, Putnam develops the beginning of an appreciation for an 'anthropological', social view of various 'subjective' phenomena in this paper.
55 G.P. Moore, 'Mathematical techniques for studying information processing by the nervous system'. In H.M. Pinsker and W.D. Willis

Jr. (eds.), *Information Processing in the Nervous System* (Raven Press, N.Y., 1980).

56 Wittgenstein, *PI*, paras 28–30.

57 Dretske, *Knowledge and the Flow of Information*, p. 7.

58 John Heil, 'Does Cognitive Psychology Rest on a Mistake?', *Mind*, Vol. XC, No. 359, July 1981, p. 331.

59 For an excellent account of this in relatively non-technical terms, see Joseph Weizenbaum, 'How Computers Work' in his *Computer Power and Human Reason* (W.H. Freeman & Co., San Francisco, 1976).

4

Knowledge of Mind

There can be no doubt about the impact of Wittgenstein's later writings upon a wide range of topics relevant to the construction of a sociology of mind. For, unlike Mead, whose lectures and writings on mind and self are justifiably celebrated among sociologists, his project enabled him to work through the ramifications of a social conception of the mental by examining an array of mental predicates in terms of their public conditions of acquisition and use. Whereas Mead had largely restricted his analyses to 'thought', 'reflection', 'consciousness', 'self' and one or two kindred concepts, Wittgenstein's work in philosophy of psychology spanned immensely many categories and predicates of mind and experience. Among his varied contributions to the refutation of Cartesian, psychologistic, 'subjectivist' and individualist preconceptions and theories about the nature of mind, there are several especially pertinent discussions which can serve to animate a specifically sociological direction of study. First, there is the famous but much misunderstood deployment of the quasi-technical notions of 'criteria' and 'criterial satisfaction' in his thinking about the intelligibility of the mental. We have already appealed to these analytical ideas in the context of the argument against the possibility of a 'private mental language'. Secondly, we must consider his profoundly consequential distinction between 'expression' and 'description' in relation to the mental and experiential domains, and the emergence of a novel framework for explicating how socialization into a mastery of public mental-and-experiential-linguistic resources is carried on.

In what follows, then, I shall attempt to enlarge upon the picture which Wittgenstein sketched for us, and indicate some areas in which misunderstandings of these matters have arisen, focusing in particular on the misleading idea that Wittgenstein was elucidating a 'folk psychology' with its own theoretical commitments.

'Criteria' and the Availability of the 'Inner'

In his discussion of 'grammar', Wittgenstein observes that what a concept means can only be determined by examining its rules of use in normal circumstances. Here, he is implicitly contrasting 'use' to 'misuse'. We learn to use words and phrases, which express particular concepts, in utterances which in turn are made intelligible and appropriate in particular kinds of contexts or occasions of communicating with one another. Some concepts, e.g. color-concepts such as 'red', are acquired on the basis of ostensive explanations involving paradigmatic samples of (red) objects, contrasting ostensions involving things colored differently, practices of locating and fetching things that are red, responding to instructions to bring something 'red', arranging objects according to their color, justifying one's application of 'red' by indicating the right sample, etc. according to the standards laid down by communication community members. The practices and standards sustained and enforced by competent trainers and teachers, including *but not restricted to* their ostensive explanations, lay down the rules for the use of such a concept, the proper ways in which this color can be named, discriminated, contrasted and in other ways enter into anyone's repertoire of intelligible-acceptable usages and socialized knowledge. Concepts like 'table', 'house', 'flower', etc. are transmitted in these ways. Other concepts, such as 'promise', 'mistake', 'stepmother', 'game', etc. cannot be taught in these ways, but require the provision, depending on the concept in question, of 'definitions', 'paraphrases', 'sets of examples', instances with 'etc.' provisions appended, and so on. All such explanations of (the meanings of) concepts furnish diverse kinds of rules of use, and are thus all contributions to their grammars. But how are the concepts of mental/experiential phenomena acquired and used? It is in this connection that Wittgenstein, as we saw from the discussion of 'subjective sovereignty', introduces and elaborates his notion of 'criteria'.

For a variety of concepts, and paradigmatically (but not exclusively) for those of the phenomena of mind, no ostensive explanations, definitions or other cognate kinds of instructional or pedagogical devices (of the sort outlined above in connection with color-concepts, for example) can be used to secure someone's acquisition of them. This is not because they are 'private' in the sense of being publicly unavailable, housed in an essentially hidden location, but because they are conceptually constituted by 'criteria'. It is certainly true that one does not 'see' another's pain, *nor does one fail to see it*, but rather one sees *that* someone is in pain or has a pain; one doesn't observe someone's 'understanding', but rather *that* he understands; one doesn't witness someone else's 'dream' but rather learns *that* (and what) he dreamt. These are grammatical remarks, not statements about the observational limitations of human beings in respect of the mental (nor comments upon the essential 'inscrutability' of mental phenomena) any more than the remark that 'bachelors are unmarried men' specifies some kind of inductively arrived at and potentially refutable 'empirical regularity' about bachelors, or any more than the claim that one's left hand cannot give one's right hand a gift exhibits a peculiar sort of (physical?) limitation on the range of human behavior[1].

How, then, *do* 'criteria' operate to provide for the sense of, and hence the availability (determinability, recognizability) of, things like 'dreams', 'mental images', 'silent thoughts' and other apparently 'inner' phenomena conventionally associated with the 'operations of the mind'? At first, it appears as though the argument which Wittgenstein makes, that the 'inner' stands in need of 'outward criteria'[2], amounts to no more than positing a general requirement for *conventional evidence(s)* for the various 'mental' phenomena. Thus, when we read him saying such things as: 'What is the criterion for the sameness of two images? – What is the criterion for the redness of an image? For me, when it is someone else's image: what he says and does'[2], it can appear as though a 'criterion' consists in forms of situated behavioral displays or claims, themselves quite other than the phenomena in question (e.g. the actual 'images' themselves) for which they can, at best, merely function as circumstantial evidences, associated with but only defeasibly connected to what they are evidences *of*. Their 'defeasibility' of connection is manifested, *inter alia*, in the observation that it is only in certain kinds of circumstances that my moaning and holding my limb amounts to 'pain-behavior' and is thus grounds for your correctly saying of me that I am in pain; alter the circumstances, and such a claim could be defeated as I can be found instead to be acting, feigning, joking, etc. In what sense, then, could moaning or writhing or avowing that one is in pain constitute 'criteria' for being in pain? At best, they appear to be weak, inductive, context-dependent evidences, scarcely enough to warrant the claim that 'criteria' (of such kinds) *define (or partly define) what it is* to be in pain, as Wittgenstein is taken to have believed.[4] Indeed, in the case of 'pain' and the supposedly criterial role of 'pain-behavior', Wittgenstein himself anticipated the possible objection that he had succumbed to a behavioristic reduction:

'But you will surely admit that there is a difference between pain-behavior accompanied by pain and pain-behavior without pain?' – Admit it? What greater difference could there be?. . .

'Are you not really a behaviorist in disguise? Aren't you at bottom really saying that everything except human behavior is a fiction?' – If I do speak of a fiction, then it is of a *grammatical* fiction.[5]

This is, on its surface, an immensely obscure claim to make, for it seems as though we are to treat something like a pain, or a mental image, as somehow less 'real' than the conduct which evinces them.

This impression is mistaken – for Wittgenstein is *not* saying that pains or mental images are themselves 'grammatical fictions', only that our tendency is to think of them as if our concepts of them operated in language along lines analogous to concepts such as (material) 'sparks' or 'flashes', or 'photographs' or 'screen-images' – still, it scarcely seems to stave off the objection about the possibly behavioristic reduction or eliminationism of the 'mental' or 'experiential' elements of our existence in the discussion of 'criteria'.

To make matters worse, we find Wittgenstein noting that 'criteria' are to be distinguished from inductive evidences (of the sort he calls 'symptoms' of the presence of a phenomenon), and are fixed by grammatical conventions.[6] Is he, then, saying that 'pains', 'mental images', 'dreams' and the like are inaccessible, and that only their behavioral and circumstantial evidences count to determine their meaning? And, even if this is conceded, what *kind* of evidences can he mean if a 'criterion' is to be *distinguished from* an inductively established regularity constituting merely an empirical 'symptom' of a phenomenon?

The way out of these knots, and the path to a richer appreciation of the insights which Wittgenstein offers to us, involves grasping the deep relationships he discerned between the 'logical' and the 'contingent', between 'grammar' and 'forms of life', between 'criteria' (as indeed components of grammar) and phenomena. A first step is to note that for anything to count as an inductively correlated piece of evidence for something (e.g. a 'symptom' of X, in Wittgenstein's terms), there must be some way of telling what X is *independently* of the identification of what counts as 'evidence' for it. After all, for Y to count as *evidence* for X presupposes the identifiability of X in the first place. Footprints in the snow can count as evidence of the presence of a prowler, but, on actually coming face-to-face with the prowler, one is no longer witnessing 'evidences' of him. There cannot be phenomena which consist purely in evidences-for-themselves! But this does *not* mean that something which in one context can count as 'evidence-for' cannot, in some different context, count as a criterion for X. In circumstances of language-training with children, one may invoke as 'criteria' what, elsewhere, for different purposes, one cites as evidence. Take the case of teaching a child the meaning of 'dream'. Wittgenstein has this to say:

> People who on waking tell us certain incidents (that they have been in such-and-such places, etc.) . . . . Then we teach them the expression 'I dreamt' which *precedes the narrative*. Afterwards I sometimes ask them 'did you dream anything last night?' and am answered yes or no, sometimes with an account of a dream, sometimes not.[7]

In such a scenario, one can see how the child's report upon waking is treated as a criterion for his having dreamt, and is used in the process of training him in a new use of language, in the use of the concept of 'dream' and of 'dreaming'. However, elsewhere, one may hear someone reporting upon his apparent nocturnal adventures and treat that merely as possible evidence for his having dreamt when, for example, there are other reasons for doubting whether he did so (e.g. the REM print-out is negative, or he has been known to wander abroad at night, get drunk, return almost comatose and fall into a deep sleep, after which he wakes up and reports upon his wanderings as if they had been a dream). Before anyone can mistake a case of real nocturnal experiences for having merely dreamt, he must have mastered the concept of what it is to dream, and such a concept can only be inculcated by criteria of the kind which, elsewhere, may count only as evidence. As Cavell put it, 'Criteria do not determine the certainty of statements, but the application of the concepts employed in statements'.[8] However, whilst it is true that 'telling that someone dreamt' depends upon mastery of the criteria (and there may be several) for the use of the concept of 'dream', and that any such criteria (such as the availability of a dream-report) may 'turn out' not to have been satisfied in some particular case (e.g. the apparently truthful dream-report was a deception for ulterior purposes), none the less, it is only by appealing to such avowals that one could 'tell' in some instance what it *was* another was characterizing in giving you his account. The dream *is* accessible – through the ratified dream-report. To switch the example for a moment back to 'pain', it is clear that moaning, groaning, screaming, writhing about and a variety of other displays figure in the adducing of criteria for what pain is, for what can *count as* someone's being in pain, even though in some circumstances such displays do not secure one's certainty as to the presence of pain. Yet, as Cavell observes, for characterizations such as 'He's feigning' or 'He's rehearsing' or 'It's a hoax' to satisfy us as explanations for someone's *not* being in pain we rely upon the criteria for pain:

> [W]hat he is feigning must be precisely *pain*, what he is rehearsing must be the part of a man *in pain*, the hoax depends on his simulating *pain*, etc. These circumstances are ones in appealing to which, in describing which, we *retain the concept* (here, of pain) whose application these criteria determine . . . . It is because of *that* satisfaction [of the criteria for pain] that we know that he is feigning pain (i.e., that it is pain he is feigning) . . .[9]

But doesn't this reasoning still permit us to drive a wedge between a 'criterion' (e.g. a sincere or truthfully offered dream-report) and the thing for which it stands as a criterion (viz. a dream)? In a sense, this is true, for the presence of criteria, like evidences, for X, does not invariantly entail X. But there is a sense in which to say this is radically to mislead. For it pushes us in the direction of wanting to claim that our not actually *seeing* someone else's dream *as he dreams it* (or our not actually feeling someone's pain in our own body – or even in his(!) – as he writhes about) leaves us bereft of anything like a warrant or justification for the correctness of an ascription of such predicates, so that we must, it appears, rest content with 'mere' *external indices* and thus corrigible inferential grounds (whether purely behavioral or a variable blend of multiple forms of behavior-and-circumstances) for really 'internal' phenomena. What Wittgenstein appeared to condemn as 'grammatical fictions' can so easily return to haunt us. It is perfectly true that no one sees another's dream as he dreams it, nor conjures up another's (undisclosed) mental image as he visualizes something to himself, nor feels another's pain (except metaphorically) as he experiences it then and there (although one can feel the *same* pain as someone else!). But this does not amount to an argument in support of the claim that criteria, given in language-training or in justifications of ascriptions for such predicates, afford only 'inferential' and not *decisive*, grounds. It is here where Wittgenstein's talk about 'grammatical fictions' has its point, because what underlies such a claim about criteria as consisting solely in inferential (and therefore *not* decisive) grounds is the tacit assumption that the 'inner experience itself' is the final arbiter of a correct ascription. Wittgenstein certainly does not want to deny that pains, for instance, are 'inner experiences', although, as we have seen, he has excellent arguments for denying that they are privately inscrutable phenomena. He says that he can barely imagine a greater difference than the occurrence of 'pain-behavior' without pain and its occurrence with pain, as we quoted him earlier. What he does want to deny in this connection is the idea that the satisfaction of the kind of things he describes as 'criteria' can *never* confer certainty upon ascriptions of mental or experiential predicates. He wants to deny that all such criterial satisfactions accomplish is the making probable of an *hypothesis* (about the presence of pain, the occurrence of a mental image or a dream, etc.). Hacker proposes the following useful analysis:

If the criteria for *q* are satisfied, i.e., if *p* is the case *in these circumstances*, then it is certain that *q*. If someone touches a red-hot poker and screams, hugs his burned hand, etc., then it is certain that he has hurt himself. 'I can be as *certain* of someone else's sensation as of any fact' (*PI*, p. 224). We could perhaps imagine *different* circumstances in which this behavior would be compatible with the person's not being in pain, but it does not follow that in these circumstances there could be any intelligible doubt. "But, if you are *certain*, isn't it that you are shutting your eyes in the face of doubt?' – 'They are shut". (Ibid.) Doubt, in such circumstances, would betoken a failure of understanding, lack of mastery of the concept of pain, not admirable caution.'[10]

What one seeks, if one *does* have grounds for doubt in a given context, is not access to some internal or 'transcendental' phenomena, but further information about the circumstances relevant to the given case at hand. And, in order to know whether or when one has sufficient evidence to make a judgement about an originally doubtful instance, one must know what *kind* of evidence one should be seeking, what sort of evidence would illuminate the case. Knowledge of criteria operates in such circumstances to govern one's empirical search-procedure(s). But not all instances can be ones in which doubt has a place: to (be able to) doubt that X is the case presupposes independent criteria for telling what counts as X. But couldn't it always be possible that a dreamer's report of his dream, for instance, was based upon an undetected error of memory? 'The question whether the dreamer's memory deceives him when he reports the dream after waking cannot arise, unless indeed we introduce a completely new criterion for the report's "agreeing" with the dream, a criterion which gives us a concept of "truth" as distinct from 'truthfulness' here.'[11] Elsewhere, discussing 'silent thoughts', Wittgenstein observes that the criteria for the truth of the confession that I thought such-and-such (say, in the context of a game of 'guessing thoughts') are not the criteria for the true *description* of any *inner process*. Rather, in such cases, there are 'special criteria of *truthfulness*'.[12] What can generate *meaningful* doubt about a disclosure which someone makes of their 'silent thoughts' is not any general metaphysic about the inaccessibility of the 'inner mental world' of others, but such practical matters as grounds for suspecting concealment, for ascribing 'bad character', for wondering about the apparent discrepancy between the supposedly revealed 'thoughts' and the rest of what is relevantly known about the one making the 'disclosure', etc. But note that, for children acquiring the concepts of 'dreams', 'mental images', 'silent thoughts', the possibility of *un*truthfulness does not arise at the outset, but can only arise later, after their spontaneous conduct and avowals have facilitated their learning such concepts for use in their own case. 'A child has much to learn before it can pretend.'[13] Here, then, is a fundamental connection between 'grammar' – the rules for the use of concepts – and 'forms of life': in this case, between the 'grammar' of much of our talk of dreams, images and the like, and the *natural* behavior of infants. Our grammars of these concepts are the way they are in part because of the natural proclivities and behavioral possibilities of human beings *prior to and as they are in the process of learning to speak of anything at all.* For example, as we saw, no concept of 'pain' could even be possible were it not for the occurrence of pre-linguistic, natural modes of public pain *expression* on the part of infants. This is not to assume that socializing agents only base their contributions to a child's acculturation in this facet of life upon their natural pain-expressions as *givens*. Attempts may be made to modify these very forms of such pre-linguistic pain-behaviors themselves in efforts to establish what may be called 'normative thresholds' for socially acceptable reactions-to-pains-of-type-X. For example, the infant who shrieks protractedly after receiving a prick from a pin in a part of the body normatively construed as relatively 'less sensitive to pain' than other parts may find him/herself subject to sanctions of varyingly punitive kinds against (what is being experienced by the socializer as) an exhibition of an excessive response.

In our discussion of the anti-'private language' argument in the last chapter, it was asserted that Wittgenstein denied that we learn to identify our own sensations and other, 'mental', phenomena on the basis of criteria. We are taught criteria for the attribution of mental and experiential predicates to others in a variety of ways, but we do not learn criteria for our own initial first-person uses of such predicates. This is the basis of the widely discussed 'asymmetry' thesis, according to which first-person uses differ from second-and third-person uses of such predicates in virtue of the different role played by 'criteria'. This thesis should not be confused with the mistaken idea that criterial *satisfaction* is irrelevant to first-person uses. Indeed, one's avowals, produced without using criteria, become *themselves* (among the various) criteria the satisfaction of which others can appeal to or subsequently use in ratifying the intelligibility, truthfulness or appropriateness of any claim about our 'psychological' status.

'Expressing' and 'Describing' the Mental

There are many sources for the temptation to think that concepts such as 'dream', 'mental image' and 'silent thought', (and the list could be extended) can be used as names of discriminable *objects* in descriptions. We say such things as: 'I've a dull, throbbing pain in my side'; 'I had an especially vivid dream last night', or 'A sudden thought popped into my head'. Such locutions have a common form with descriptive ones such as: 'I've a cracked tooth'; 'I had a beautiful photograph of you', or 'The rabbit popped out of the hat', in which the 'have' is that of possession and what is (or was) possessed is an object, or in which a sudden event occurs involving an object. This commonality of form can easily suggest a misassimilation of otherwise quite diverse kinds of expression to one type, where the error is to consider the meanings of the expressions apart from their (greatly differing) contexts of possible *use*, as if commonality of form was an invariant key to commonality of sense. Without an examination of the 'grammars' of the concepts involved, and this involves a consideration of the sorts of contexts appropriate to the expressions within which such concepts can intelligibly be employed, one can be misled into thinking that, since pains, dreams and thoughts are clearly not *material* objects, they *must* be mental objects. Moreover, confusions can ramify: if they are mental objects, then we must use some 'inner sense' to 'perceive' them (cf. the doctrine of introspectionism), and when we speak of their occurring we must be 'describing' them on the basis of that 'internal' perception.

A first step in unravelling these misconceptions consists in noticing that, in the case of 'the dream' and 'the thought' we have corresponding verbs, '(to) dream (dreaming)' and 'to (have) thought'. We do not (idiomatic usage aside) have a verb for 'pain' such as 'paining', but we do have very closely related ones like 'hurting', 'aching', and so on. We shall postpone consideration of 'pain' for a moment, and focus our attention on 'dream' and 'thought'. To say that one 'had a dream' is to say *no more than* that one 'dreamt' something, and to say that one 'had a sudden thought' is to say *no more than* that one suddenly 'thought' of or about something. Notice that there can be no such thing as having a 'dream' or a 'thought' in and of itself, so to speak, apart from what it is a dream or a thought *of* or *about*, in such expressions as these. Such a feature of usage is sometimes referred to as the 'intentionality of the mental', following Brentano's (and Husserl's) well-known phrase. In other words, unlike 'tables', 'flowers' or 'automobiles', 'dreams' and 'thoughts' are necessarily *of or about something* (to name only two of the complementizers) – they 'take objects' *essentially*, even if tacitly. A question such as: 'What *of*?' or 'What *about*?' is always a possibly intelligible option for a hearer upon being told by a speaker simply that he had a dream or a (sudden) thought. Such is *not* an intelligible question to raise on being informed by someone that he possesses, e.g. a car, some money or a loaf of bread, although it *can* be asked of someone who says that he owns a picture or a painting, both of which *are* material objects. A 'picture' or a 'painting' is, often *of* something (but *not necessarily*: think of abstract art). However, the verb-equivalents of such *representational* objects as these, viz. '(to) picture' and '(to) paint', do not have the same necessary relationship to the one who is their subject. If I have a dream or a sudden thought, then it is *I* who dream(t) of *X* or suddenly thought about *Y* or of *Y necessarily*. On the other hand, if I have a picture or a painting of something, this does not *entail* that it is or was *I* who pictured or painted that something.

The case of pain is slightly less tractable to such an analysis, but then it is perhaps less intuitively tempting to say of pains anyway that they are objects of *any* kind. Although we do speak about the *location* of pains, as we may speak of the locations of most objects, we do not assume them to have some (unknown) shape or color, some (unknown) length or density, some (unknown) thickness or weight, taste or fragrance, or component parts. But if we say that we have 'a dull, throbbing pain' and specify a location, and a duration, for such a pain, surely we are describing *something*? Are we not attributing properties (dullness, throbbing) to some-*thing*?

Wittgenstein argued strongly against such an intuition. His first move is to note that our socialization into the language-games involving the word 'pain' depends upon our being coaxed to substitute the *linguistic reaction* of 'It hurts!', 'Pain!' or 'I've a pain' ('I'm in pain', etc.) for the natural, *pre*-linguistic reactions consisting in cries, groans, etc. *when* one has been injured in some way. After such a spontaneous *verbal* reaction has been inculcated, further articulations can be taught to the infant. The use of 'I have (a) pain' and its cognates is '*rooted* in natural pain-behavior, but what grows from this differs as the foliage of a tree from its roots',[14] as Hacker says. In coming to be able to say something as relatively elaborate as: 'I've a dull, throbbing pain in my left side', a language-user must clearly already have mastered the more elementary uses of 'pain' in making learned linguistic substitutions for natural, pre-linguistic pain-reactions.[15] It is not that he first learns to 'identify' something inside him to which he can properly refer with the use of the word 'pain'. He simply is taught a *linguistic* form of pain-response or pain-behavior. The more elaborate locutions may be regarded, however, as more akin to 'reports' than to 'linguistic reactions'. But are such reports *descriptions* of something? Granting that a locution such as: 'I have pain!' can be a linguistic *expression-of-pain*, rather than a 'description' of something, it appears arbitrarily to stretch the notion of an 'expression' and diminish the notion of 'description' to affirm only that the longer locution ('I have a dull, throbbing pain in my left side') is an extended expression (like a lengthy but reticulated cry!) and not a description. The point to note here is that, whilst we may call such a locution a description, it is better characterized as a *complaint* for many purposes of its production. However, a physician may perfectly well ask one to 'describe your pain', and may be satisfied with such a locution as a response to his solicitation, so we seem to be constrained to allow that, for at least *some* contexts, such a locution can function as a description. If it can be a description, then, it is a description of something – but of what? At this point, the argument appears to have come round full circle, even if the circle has been considerably narrowed.

Consider, then, the following. I may say: 'I've a dull pain' or 'I've a throbbing pain'. But I can equally well say that I have a (very) unpleasant *leaden feeling*, or a *painful throbbing*, or that my leg is '*burning* (*stinging, nagging, searing*, etc.) *with* pain'. Here, the use of 'pain' as the accusative 'object' disappears, even though what is expressed by such paraphrases as these loses none of the meaning conveyed by those expressions in which 'pain' does figure as the noun in 'grammatical-object' position. But how can we come to be able to describe our 'throbbings', 'burnings', 'searings', 'stingings' if not by observing our sensations and finding them to satisfy such descriptions? The problem has shifted from 'pains' but only to be replaced by a similar problem concerning the nominalised versions of some of the adjectives that can qualify them. Ryle, however, offered the following important clue:

When a sufferer describes a pain as a stabbing, a grinding, or a burning pain, though he does not necessarily think that his pain is given to him by a stiletto, a drill, or an ember, still he says what sort of a pain it is by likening it to the sort of pain that would be given to anyone by such instruments. . . . We do not employ a 'neat' sensation vocabulary. We describe particular sensations by referring to how common objects regularly look, sound and feel to any normal person.[16]

In order to achieve this, however, one must be trained by others during the acquisition of language to utter the right words under the right circumstances, and these will involve unpleasant encounters with various common objects. Someone who has never had a nasty physical encounter with fire or with hot objects cannot acquire the concept of a 'burning (pain, sensation)' for later first-person use *in the absence of fire*. But how could someone learn to describe a pain later as 'burning', say, in circumstances where no very hot object is involved? It seems as though he would have to remember his previous pain experienced in circumstances involving fire or a hot object and make a comparison with his present experience in order properly to describe it in such terms. If someone remembers something, and can make a comparison between it and something else, surely that achievement presupposes *observation* of the thing compared? Here we can enter a straightforward denial. Remembering and comparing sensations do *not* entail having observed or observing them. Neither do they entail perceiving them. We do not observe or perceive 'pains' (or 'burning sensations', etc.):

I do not observe or perceive my own experiences . . . I *have* them. If it made sense for a person to perceive his own experiences, then it would make sense to misperceive them. Then we could understand what it would be for someone to have severe pain but not to have observed it, or for him to seem to himself to perceive great pain but for there to be no pain at all. But this is perspicuously nonsense; *these are not possibilities which do not happen to occur*, but forms of words that are excluded from language, that have no roles as descriptions of possibilities.[17]

And, as Ryle remarks: 'Observing is finding out, or trying to find out, something, but having a sensation is neither finding out, nor trying to find out, nor failing to find out, anything.'[18] And this holds not just for experiences such as having pains, but for 'mental' processes and events such as dreaming, having mental images or sudden thoughts. I do not 'observe myself' dreaming, conjuring up an image, or having a sudden thought; I have dreams, have mental images and think my thoughts. My remembering, recollecting, comparing or 'likening' dreams, thoughts, images or pains cannot, then, involve observations of such things on my part: my remembering a pain is grammatically equivalent to my remembering *that I was in pain*, and my capacity to 'compare' a pain (a dream, an image, etc.) involves the exercise of my capacity to specify what it is like now in terms of what it was like then. Being able to 'play' the language-game(s) of likening sensations to other ones involves having been taught in originary circumstances during linguistic socialization what to say of one's pain (etc.) in those circumstances. Thus, e.g., a child is burned playing with matches and is told that what it is experiencing is a 'burn', 'burning pain', or their cognates. This use of language can then form part of the recollection that one was in pain such that one can recollect that one was in pain *in that particular way*. There is no logical requirement for 'observation' even to enter the depiction.

Assimilating varieties of experiential expressions to one common, formal type can, then, incur mistakes about the nature of what is depicted. Concepts like 'dream', 'mental image', 'thought' and 'pain', although diverse in many obvious respects, may come to be characterized as, or assumed to be, concepts for (peculiar kinds of) mental/experiential entities. As such, they may be thought of as 'observed' (in a supremely 'private' sense) and 'described' on the basis of observation of their inherently perceivable 'natures', such internal perception being 'privileged' and effected by the operation of some interior analogue to the corporeal 'senses'. What is forgotten is the root of experiential 'naming' and 'description' in forms of linguistic-behavioral training which itself depends upon infant 'expressive' propensities which differ according to the experiential circumstances encountered. Without a natural and necessarily pre-linguistic range of public reactions to pains of different kinds, *linguistic* reactions could not be imparted and subsequently elaborated upon. Without spontaneous accounts of putative nocturnal experiences delivered by children upon awakening from sleep, dream-reports could not be constituted as such for them, and so on. To ignore the pivotal role of such phenomena is to ignore the social processes whereby any mental domain can be conceptualized. It is to court misconceptions of the mental and experiential life in which it is held that because aspects of such a life are indeed 'inner' they are only truly accessible, 'observable', describable by virtue of conjectural subjective-introspective processes.

It is not just an affliction of theorists but perhaps of a particular form of theorizing as such (whether lay or professional) to entertain such misconceptions of the mental/experiential domains as we have been arguing against. The de-reification of the products of such 'theorizing' is a necessary preliminary to, and an essential aspect of, a properly socio-logical inquiry into these topics.

Is Our Mental/Experiential Language Essentially 'Theoretical'?

Several contemporary philosophical commentators on the question of the nature of our knowledge of mind have argued that our so-called 'ordinary language' in fact embodies either a 'theory of mind' or, at least, certain 'theoretical assumptions'. Further, if this is conceded, then so is the possibility that any such theory or theoretical assumptions might turn out to be false. And, indeed, some commentators have tried to argue exactly this. Aune offers the following argument:[19]

Consider the term 'lunatic'. In its original sense this term *meant* 'a person whose madness has a lunar cause'. In this sense of the term, there is a conceptual connection between lunacy and the moon, one reflected in the conceptual truth that x is a lunatic just in case x's madness is caused by the moon. But if, in fact, the moon does not cause a kind of madness – as we now believe – there is no factual basis for applying the word 'lunatic' to any person and, therefore, for using the word in its original sense. The same holds true for words such as 'feels pain' or 'is dizzy'.

Aune goes on to claim that, since there must be some factual basis to any conceptual truth, we need inductively ascertained empirical evidence to support such 'truths'. Our practical reasoning with 'criteria' for the mental must do 'justice to the kind of reasoning common in theoretical science'.[20] I would propose, however, that a concept like 'lunacy' has only a *partially* theoretical genealogy. Unlike 'phlogiston', for example, which nowadays we would regard as having no proper referent at all, we can and do still use the concept of 'lunacy' and 'lunatic' in our practical affairs to identify or in other ways speak of craziness, madness, insanity and persons so afflicted. When we do talk this way, we no longer presuppose the sort of hypothesized connection between madness and the moon's phases which once informed our common reasoning about insanity. Yet a part of the meaning of the original concept remains intact: roughly speaking, a 'lunatic' is still a (currently colloquial and pejorative) term for someone who is mad, and *this* aspect of its sense is preserved, just as we may characterize someone quite intelligibly as 'melancholic' without presupposing that aspect of its original sense in which the bile theory of the humors was involved.

Our practical employment of the language of mind expresses *concepts*, and concepts, unlike *theories* or theoretical propositions, are neither true nor false: they may be misused, wrongly explained or inappropriately invoked for certain purposes in specific circumstances, but if they have currency and rules of use, then it follows that they can be employed to make sense. Aune does not venture any supposedly 'theoretical' genealogy for the concepts of 'pain' and 'dizziness' (nor for 'feels', either), all of which he groups together as sharing this property with 'lunacy'. Dennett, however, locates different grounds for supposing that 'the *attribute, being-in-pain*, is not a well-behaved theoretical attribute'[21], and he claims that 'our everyday attributions in mentalistic or intentional language' is a 'mess'.[22] In advancing these claims, Dennett produces arguments such as the following:

A textbook announces that nitrous oxide renders one 'insensible to pain', a perfectly ordinary turn of phrase which elicits no 'deviancy' startle in the acutest ear, but it suggests that nitrous oxide doesn't prevent the occurrence of pain at all, but merely makes one insensible to it when it does occur (as one can be rendered insensible to the occurrence of flashing lights by a good blindfold). Yet the same book classifies nitrous oxide among analgesics, that is *preventers* of pain (one might say 'painkillers') and we do not bat an eye.[23]

Commenting upon this move, Malcolm diagnoses the problem to lie not with the ordinary meaning of 'pain', nor with its putatively ill-behaved character as a theoretical concept (which it is not), but with Dennett's own inability to distinguish between a form of words and how that form of words is used.[24] The assumption that the phrase 'insensible to . . .' must have the same meaning in every context leads Dennett wrongly to assimilate 'insensible to pain' to 'insensible to the occurrence of a flashing light'. In the latter usage, one may very well propose that the flashing light was still there to be seen, but if one is rendered 'insensible to pain', there is no reason to propose that the pain was somehow still there to be felt: being rendered insensible to pain is preventing one's pain from occurring. Dennett presses his charge about the 'incoherence' of our ordinary concept of 'pain' by noting that, in cases of prefrontal lobotomy, patients sometimes say that they are still in pain but they 'seem and claim not to *mind*'[25] the pain. Armstrong comments on this phenomenon also in saying of such patients that 'It seems as if they are saying that they have a pain which is giving them no pain!'[26] Malcolm's reply to both contentions is simply to agree that the phenomenon is strange, but that its strangeness arises precisely because of the normal contrast we all make between saying that a pain is intense and saying that one doesn't mind it being so. If a patient displays no pain-reaction whatsoever whilst affirming the intensity of pain, then one 'would not understand what he is saying'.[27] Malcolm's argument boils down to warning us not to treat the confusions of particular speakers as indices of 'confusions' somehow inherent in the language spoken, as if a natural language were *ab initio* a repository of theoretical claims rather than of conceptual resources (for theorizing, but also for *many* other pursuits).

In the course of a rebuttal to Malcolm, Armstrong remarks that there is a danger in construing the pain-and-pain-behavior relation as a grammatical one because 'pain and its behavioral expression are "distinct existences" in Hume's sense', and he adds: 'If this distinctness of existence is doubted, then the case of curare-induced paralysis should put it beyond doubt. The paralyzed person can be in great pain, yet behavioral expression be completely denied to him'.[28] It is worth recalling here Wittgenstein's acknowledgement that 'pain' and 'pain-behavior' are indeed different, because one can encounter circumstances in which either occurs without the other: the point is, however, that pain-behavior *in certain circumstances* is a criterion (and neither inductive nor deductive *evidence*) for pain. Without acknowledging this criterial connection within grammar, there is no way to explain *anyone's* possession of this concept in the first place. Such a criterial connection, as noted, is not an entailment relation; the curare case raised by Armstrong is not evidence in support of the contention that pain and pain-behavior are 'distinct existences' in the sense that they are only inductively correlatable but otherwise wholly different things. After all, we are talking about pain's relationship to '*pain*-behavior', not to any old behavior!

Moreover, how is Armstrong (or anyone) in a position to say of the curare-induced paralytic that he is in pain unless in *some* circumstances some such victim of curare poisoning has *avowed or displayed as much* and in *those* circumstances has been heard to be speaking *truthfully*? It is certainly true that we can be misled by stoicism as much as by feigned 'pains' into occasional misattributions. In the case of the paralytic suffering from unexpressible pain, we may well face the prospect of making mistakes – even cruel mistakes – but if we know from past encounters (*within which the criteria for attribution have been met, e.g. a truthful avowal*) that a given cause for the condition prevails (e.g. curare poisoning), we can use this as a *new criterion* for attributing pain in the absence of observable reactions to it on the part of the sufferer. It may be proposed that, here, we invoke a theoretical criterion for making an attribution. It seems to me, however, that, if something is well-established knowledge, it can serve just as well as a practical criterion: there is nothing theoretical about the capacity of curare to cause pain, although in some given instances of curare poisoning such a capacity may not be known or may not even be in effect. Criteria are neither static nor metaphysical guarantors of certainty for all cases; this does not mean that they are to be construed generically as merely 'theoretical', 'inferential' or 'probabilifying' in all cases, either.

These observations are in no sense intended as contributions to something referred to in recent literature as 'folk psychology'[29]. In so far as there is such a thing, it would presumably consist in more or less widely held substantive beliefs about mind and the mental, personality and the 'proper' explanation of conduct in some general sense. Our topic in this discussion has not been concerned with whatever forms of 'lay psychological *theorizing*' may be abroad; on the contrary, and herein lies a critical distinction, our focus has been upon various aspects of *practical* 'psychological' *reasoning*, our everyday *pre*-theoretical *conceptualisations* of the mental and experiential as they enter into and inform the lives we lead as members of a culture and natural-language community.

There is some suspicion abroad in much contemporary philosophy of the notion of an 'ordinary' or 'pre-theoretical' language of the mental. For example, we have seen how some philosophers claim to find theoretical genealogies for some of our commonly acquired and used concepts in this domain, arguing that such genealogies for them somehow render our mundane language-games involving them either 'scientifically corrigible' or else downright 'defective' as instruments of reason and communication. Enough has been said about these misconceptions for the moment. Others argue that the whole notion of 'ordinariness' in respect of language is misplaced, and that, therefore, appeals to 'ordinary, pre-theoretical language-games' cannot inform, much less constrain, 'scientific' approaches to cognition: what is 'ordinary' language-use in reference to minds and the mental for the psychiatric clinician or theorist of cognitive science is hardly 'ordinary' to the janitor or the taxi-driver[30]. Here we must be very careful to specify the parameters of the type of 'ordinariness' in question (and we should avoid assigning 'ordinary language-use' exclusively to some vague category of 'ordinary people'!). For whilst it is perfectly true that a 'technical language' can become so routinized among professionals as to be 'ordinary' to them, no one seriously argues (do they?) that technical categories such as 'ego dysfunction' or 'neural representation' are 'ordinary' or 'mundane' usages *tout court*. Any such specialized 'language' is fundamentally a 'sub-language' differentiated out of, but retaining grammatical links to, non-technical vernacular usages. It is when attempts are made to *sever* such links that 'metaphysics' emerges as the '*disguised* nonsense' that it is. And there can be little doubt that some sciences have more than their fair share of so-called 'theoretical propositions' which are, under analysis, metaphysical pseudo-propositions.

Boundary questions always rear their heads at this juncture: where are the limits of the 'mundane language-games' and how does one demarcate the borderlines between the 'ordinary' and the 'technical', between the 'grammatically intact' and the 'metaphysically adventurous' conceptual moves? In this regard, it is worth noting that, while general boundaries cannot be precisely specified in any all-purpose fashion, their absence does not deter us, any more than the failure to locate an exact line between any two English counties entails a general inability to know when we are in Lancashire and when we are in Yorkshire. Any logico-grammatical claim, any explicatory analysis of *praxis* in daily affairs, is a piecemeal matter which depends upon the local cogency of its particulars and its arguments for the very basis of 'logic' remains 'intuitively-founded common agreement'. And, as Wittgenstein remarked, 'This seems to abolish logic, but does not do so.'[31]

The acquisition of knowledge of mind and the mental, the 'subjective' and experiential, is, we have proposed, a component part of our more general socialization, involving as it does being trained, drilled, shown, corrected, instructed and in other ways inducted into both our own society's culture as well as into 'the common behavior of mankind'.[32] Our common reactions, discriminations, judgements and forms of living enable us to develop a complex grammar of conceptualization, and this web of concepts gives us our ways of making sense of the world, including our 'subjective' attributes. Although we say of particular natural-languages (English, Spanish, Arabic, Russian, etc.) that they have 'grammars', it is important to keep in mind the more generic sense of 'grammar' we are invoking in these discussions. Given that all natural languages are, in principle, translatable (and largely in practice, too, save for those few remaining ancient languages for whose translation we lack access to common reference-points), we may properly speak of a 'grammar' of concepts as an endowment of *the species as a whole,* however any segment of mankind actually participates in its available resources.

The sort of grammatical elucidations of 'mental' concepts we have been considering thus far, then, are not idiosyncratic to any particular culture: the discussion and analysis has been conducted here in English, but could (with varying practical difficulties) be rendered in any other natural language in which the relevant concepts have a place (and it is safe to surmise that this covers all of them). (Wittgenstein developed many of them in his native German, a language with a somewhat different *syntax* from English, but a common logical grammar.) Indeed, to assume that something might exist as a language and yet be untranslatable in principle is to assume that there are no logical limits to the very concept of a 'language': for something to *count as* a language in the first place (as distinct, say, from random noises, grunts or sounds) *is* for it to be translatable, even if not actually (yet) translated. It may be empirically true to say of some small African society that 'it lacks a concept of "electron"', just as it may be true to say of some sub-cultural group within our own society that 'its members lack a concept of "electron"', but the concept of 'electron' is a piece in language-games that *can be played* within grammar, that are available for use in communicative and cognitive affairs just as much as Azande oracular 'benge' is such a piece (although perhaps few people in Outer Mongolia or the rain forests of Brazil have ever heard of it or used it in discourse). In one African tribal society, there is a concept of affect called 'lirima', and in parts of Malaya there is a mental illness called 'amok'. These concepts are not operable in routine, everyday affairs of affect-attribution or psychiatric ascriptions within our English-speaking culture: at best, they are available as topics for analytical or academic discussion. However, their meanings are knowable and, of course, known: they are governed by grammatical conventions which are determinable, and form part of the conceptual endowment of the human species, notwithstanding their differential empirical distributions of actual usage and the different kinds of language-games played with them in different cultures. To say of 'mind', then, that it is 'culturally'-constituted has been generally to speak of 'culture' in the large.

Notes

1 Cf. Wittgenstein, *PI*, para. 268.
2 Ibid., *PI*, para. 580.
3 Ibid., para. 377.
4 He is taken to have maintained this primarily on the basis of his remarks in the *Blue and Brown Books* (Basil Blackwell, Oxford, 1958), esp. p. 24, where he writes of 'criteria' in terms of '*defining* criteria', and in the *PI*, para. 354, where he seems to assume a sense of 'criterion' as definitional.
5 Wittgenstein, *PI*, paras 304, 307.
6 Wittgenstein, *Blue and Brown Books*, p. 24.
7 Wittgenstein, *PI*, p. 184, emphasis added.
8 Stanley Cavell, 'Criteria and Scepticism'. In his *The Claim of Reason* (Oxford University Press, Oxford, 1979), p. 45. Of course, this sort of reasoning is anathema to followers of Jacques Derrida, but then it strikes me that it would be a nightmare to be a neophyte acquiring language from an actually *practising* Derridean – although, it should be noted, Derrideans tend to reserve their arbitrarianisms about language for their theorizing, and presumably not for their children.
9 Ibid.

10 P.M.S. Hacker, *Insight and Illusion: Themes in the Philosophy of Wittgenstein* (Oxford University Press, Oxford; revised edition, 1986), p. 315.

11 Wittgenstein, *PI*, pp. 222–3.

12 Ibid., p. 222.

13 Ibid., p. 229.

14 Hacker, *Insight and Illusion*, p. 294.

15 Wittgenstein, *PI*, para. 244.

16 Gilbert Ryle, *The Concept of Mind* (Hutchinson, London, 1949), pp. 193–4.

17 Hacker, *Insight and Illusion*, p. 283, emphasis added.

18 Ryle, *The Concept of Mind*, p. 195.

19 Bruce Aune, 'Other Minds After Twenty Years'. In P.A. French, T.E. Uehling Jr and H.K. Wettstein (eds), *Midwest Studies in Philosophy, Vol. 10: Studies in the Philosophy of Mind* (University of Minnesota Press, Minneapolis, 1986), p. 560.

20 Ibid., p. 561.

21 D.C. Dennett, *Brainstorms* (Bradford Books, Vermont, 1978), p. xx.

22 Ibid., p. xvii.

23 Ibid., p. 221.

24 Norman Malcolm, 'Consciousness and Causality: Consciousness'. In D.M. Armstrong and N. Malcolm, *Consciousness and Causality* (Basil Blackwell, Oxford, 1985 edn), p. 11.

25 Dennett, *Brainstorms*, p. 221.

26 D.M. Armstrong, *A Materialist Theory of the Mind* (Routledge & Kegan Paul, London1968), p. 313: cited in Malcolm, *Consciousness and Causality*, p. 12.

27 Malcolm, 'Consciousness and Causality', p. 12.

28 D.M. Armstrong, 'Reply [to Malcolm]'. In Armstrong and Malcolm, *Consciousness and Causality*, p. 205.

29 Cf. Stephen Stich, *From Folk Psychology to Cognitive Science: The Case Against Belief* (MIT Press, Cambridge, Mass., 1983). For a critical assessment of Stich's views, see Meredith Williams, 'Wittgenstein's Rejection of Scientific Psychology', *Journal for the Theory of Social Behavior*, Vol. 15, No. 2, July 1985.

30 I discern this sort of argument in Alec McHoul's critical remarks in his preface to *Telling How Texts Talk: Essays on Reading and Ethnomethodology* (Routledge & Kegan Paul, London, 1982).

31 Wittgenstein, *PI*, para. 242.

32 Wittgenstein, *PI*, para. 206.

5

Praxis and Personality

It is only within organizations of sayings and doings that assignably 'personal' attributes are made manifest. Further, it is only within organizations of sayings and doings that the *activities* of personal-attribute description, ascription, avowal, inference and assessment are to be found. Their location within such organizations of sayings and doings as are mundanely and (largely) unreflectively co-produced by people living their lives, is not merely incidental to their nature. Indeed, in so far as 'no concept of context-in-general exist(s)',[1] and in so far as any enacted characterization of a person is subject to contextual and purpose-dependent relevances for its adequacy assessment, if only minimally with reference to the issue of who it is produced for (what Sacks calls the principle of 'recipient design'[2]), along with 'when' and 'why' it is produced, then it follows that *no* characterization of 'who' someone is, what his or her 'personality traits' consist in, what he or she 'essentially' is (like) as a 'person', 'character' or 'type', can be posited as *independent* of practical purpose(s) or situated, local or occasioned contingencies. These will include the abstract but particularizable 'relevances' of psychological, social-psychological, psychiatric, psychoanalytic, psychiatric-legal or other cognate brands of generic 'theorizing'.

There are many occasions in the rounds of everyday affairs which require of parties to such affairs to specify, in so many words, what someone is (like) *really*. Diagnostics, occupational chances, professional opportunities, employment prospects, electoral contests, recruitment options, dismissal proceedings, court 'character' witness assessments, *inter alia*, can hinge upon the production and ratification of such occasioned, local, purposeful judgements of 'personality', 'type', and kindred assessment practices. Moreover, the entire machinery of the professional 'psych'-disciplines (psychiatry, psychoanalysis, personality psychology, and so forth) rests assuredly upon the claim that such generalized verdicts can and must be adduced with the fullest possible impartiality, detachment and rigor available for any such essentially normative enterprise of practical reasoning.

It is not my purpose to advance any sort of generalized 'impossibility' argument with respect to the claimed *impartiality* of any 'personality' or 'character' attributions as these are undertaken in daily social affairs. My purpose here is, rather, to specify some sociological aspects of such attributional practices, and to consider their relationship to analyses of activities and their organizations *sui generis*. Before proceeding with this task, however, a number of preliminary arguments about standard *theoretical* treatments of 'personality' are required.

'Personality' as Explanatory Construct

A common practice in practical reasoning about people is the appeal to 'personality' characteristics as explanations of their activities. We routinely encounter such explanatory locutions as: 'He did it because he's an X' or: 'She said that because she's X', where X can be substituted with one or more of a wide range of natural-language predicates of personal attribute.

'Aggressive', 'industrious', 'mean', 'dignified', 'trustworthy', 'ill-tempered', 'courageous', 'neurotic' and a host of other epithets belong to this domain of the language of personal assessment, and their nominalizations or 'type' constructions[3] constitute the summary, vernacular objectifications of 'personality': 'a self-sacrificing type', 'an egomaniac', 'a compromiser', 'a coward', and so forth. In their deployment in explanatory constructions, it can seem as if the activities being explained by reference to personality *flow from* or are *caused by* the personality of the agent. It is as if there were some 'underlying' attribute or aggregate of attributes – even a 'state' – from which issue forth lines of action or styles of action and whose existence thus explains their production or manner of production.

This mode of thinking is both fallacious and misleading. It assumes that the 'because' of explanation is always causal, and posits a reification of attributes which misconstrues their grammar. Rather, personality concepts or categories express dispositions, tendencies, proclivities to act (or to refrain from acting) or to act in certain ways (under certain circumstances, *ceteris paribus*). Thus, seeing an instance of an action (or a 'refraining') or a manner of doing/saying something as explained by reference to personality is only to see that action or its manner of performance as *exhibiting* the claimed disposition or proclivity. A jealous man does not behave in a jealous fashion because some putatively underlying 'state' of jealousy compels him, but rather his behaving in a witnessably jealous fashion is an instance of his disposition or proclivity itself *on display*.

The explanation works as an explanation not by virtue of its having identified a cause of an effect but by virtue of its having identified an instance properly describable for practical purposes as, say, an 'act of jealousy' and having linked it to a (putative) pattern of such conduct on the part of the agent. It may now be found not to be, e.g., something unusual or exceptional for such a person, deserving of circumstantial reason-giving or reason-finding, but an expectable move for him. In this way, explanations of action by reference to personality can operate as *disparity-reducing devices* and delete the local relevance of circumstantial reasons; they do not function as causal accounts. Naturally, people make predictions based upon personality attributions, but these do not work nomologically. Thus, ascertaining that some specific prediction based upon a personality attribution fails does not necessarily suggest the need for revisions of the attribution (e.g. 'maybe he's not a callous/jealous/trustworthy person after all'), but rather can afford occasions to search for a reason for the conduct or its absence *independent of* the personality assessment. Although not incorrigible with respect to counter-instances, personality attributions are often extremely enduring: even when someone has afforded much evidence in his or her conduct-in-contexts to counter the attribution, it is possible to sustain it and characterize the person as, e.g., 'a reformed hypochondriac', 'a former schizophrenic', 'a lapsed radical', 'an erstwhile homosexual', and the like. On-record histories, biographies or reputations are difficult to undo, especially when they have been subjected to framing in terms of 'personality'.

'Personality' and Social Interaction

'Personalities' can be constructed out of widely diverse materials: resources as varied as first-hand, continuous observation across many different circumstances of conduct; a single 'key' instance taken to function as a 'test'; explicit avowals or declarations from the agent ratifiable by evidentiary conduct; mediated reports from differentially-placed and differentially-valued sources; *n*th-hand accounts such as rumor or gossip, and other forms of judgementally-relevant, commonsense 'data'. However, a vital ingredient in the formation and formulation of personality attributions of all kinds is the potential for 'reactive assessment' of the attributor. In finding someone to be a certain type of person in these terms, lay (and professional) judges can encounter this phenomenon in the ways in which their judgements can themselves be judged along the same dimensions. Researchers working in spouse-abuse clinics, for example, report that a curious symmetry can arise in which, e.g., the personality attribution of one spouse is matched by a counter-attribution from the other in terms which potentially undermine the original attribution by tacitly furnishing criteria for its possible defeat (and vice versa). Thus, one spouse characterizes the other as, e.g., 'a poor listener', while the other makes an attribution of 'persistent nag'. Or again, one party calls the other 'a lazy s.o.b.', while the other party calls the first a 'hyperactive bitch'. Again, one characterizes the other as 'a nervous type', and the other calls the first 'an unpredictable man'. (I am indebted to Lee Ann Hoff for this observation.) Just as 'modest' folk can find 'vanity' where others fail to see it and 'selfless' folk may detect 'selfishness' in others where still others cannot, so also do 'nervous' people detect 'courage' where others do not. The list can be extended considerably. However, although such symmetrically challenging reciprocities of assessment are perhaps relatively uncommon, personality attributors, lay and professional, occasional or consistent, confront the omnipresent possibility that their 'personalities' will show up in their assessments of the personalities of others.

In so far as 'personalities' are compounded out of modalities of activity and situations of activity over time, it is important for analysts of activities to examine the nature of the relationship(s) which obtain between them. As practical, vernacular glosses, 'personality characteristics' may be pressed into many varied forms of service in everyday affairs: as complaints, grounds for excusing, praising or blaming, bases for forming expectations or plans, explanations of particular or recurrent actions, etc., they can do sterling work in simplifying, summarizing and rendering manageable the complexities of normative conduct. As components of a theory or systematic analysis of the properties of human conduct, however, such attributions are highly problematic in a number of respects.

Consider, first, the essential distraction from a detailed concern for the logic of action and interaction entailed by such summary, evaluative glosses. The assumption that someone's conduct can be parcelled out into the 'components' due to the exigencies or normative requirements of a situation of action and the 'components' due to the nature of his or her 'personality' type makes its appearance (among other places) in the Parsonian trichotomy of social, cultural and personality 'systems' construed as more or less discretely analysable foci of human conduct. In response to this kind of reasoning, Bolton argued that 'even the few studies that provide some scanty evidence for personality stability in adulthood fail to consider the fact that regularity of personal behavior may be as readily explained by regularities in the social scheduling of behavioral performances as by persistence in personality structure.'[4] Although one cannot characterize a conditional counter-assertion as a 'fact', Bolton's point is well taken: it articulates a standard dilemma facing someone seeking to explain human conduct in generic terms. However, it should be remembered that it is not solely the occurrence or recurrence of 'behavioral performances' which is implicative for personality attributions: it can also be refrainings from behavior as well as specific aspects of *manner* of behaving, among other considerations.

The problem of relating 'personality' to the analysis of action makes itself felt with special force in the domain of formal interaction analysis. Schegloff could just as well be referring to 'personality-trait' categories when he makes the following point:

the fact that they [social interactants] are 'in fact' respectively a doctor and a patient does not make those characterisations ipso facto relevant (as is especially clear when the patient is also a doctor); their respective ages, sex, religions, and so on, or altogether idiosyncratic and ephemeral attributes (for example, 'the one who just tipped over the glass of water on the table') may be what is relevant at any point in the talk . . . . That is, there should be some tie between the context-as-characterised and its bearing on 'the doing of the talk' or 'doing the interaction'.[5]

Construing 'personal attributes' as features of 'context' enables us to exploit a distinction important for analytical purposes in any attempted explication of the logic of *praxis*: a distinction between 'context' considered as any specification of co-occurring or coexisting particulars and *member-relevant* contextual particulars. In so far as 'personal attributes' are topicalized or implied/ presupposed in courses of practical (communicative) action, they may be considered as 'member-relevant' particulars (i.e. displayed to and detected by them in and through their action(s)) in relation to the construction of those courses of action. 'Personality traits' may not be heralded as explicitly prior to interactions as may those perceptually available or emblematically revealed membership categories of other types[6] (e.g. 'black', 'male', 'police officer', 'nurse', 'priest', etc.), although indeed for those 'in the know', 'a man's reputation can march before him', thereby prefiguring various modalities of 'recipient design' practices engaged in by knowledgeable interactants/interlocutors. Although such practices as 'designing one's conduct in specific relation to Other's (presumed) personality characteristic of type X' may concretely vary in content, their generic forms are intersubjective and analysable.

Contemporary sociological thought within the interactionist perspective, with its focus upon socially allocated 'roles', whether these be construed structurally (e.g. occupational, professional or organizational 'role') or dramaturgically (after Goffman's writings about the 'presentation of self'), has tended to nurture what one might call a 'non-morbid, multiple-personalities' conception of human agents. We do not, according to such a view, possess just one personality, a relatively stable unity of perceptible character-istics, but many 'personae', each of which is comprised by the situated rationalities of conduct particular to the varying activity-structures within which and across which we navigate as social beings. It is our relationships to any or to each of these situated rationalities which provide the bases for the assignability of attributes of 'personality', and any such determination will, according to this conception, depend upon necessarily *synech-dochal* extrapolations. Such assessments will generally be subject to an often unstated defeasibility rider such as: 'of course, I only see him at work', or 'from the perspective of a friend of hers', or 'I've known him all of his life, except when he was in the army . . .', etc. Moreover, there are ordinarily 'occasioning' circumstances which make appropriate any such global or even partially summarizing attributions of personality. In this sense, for example, spontaneous and routine conformities to normative entitlements of behavior do not generate grounds for calling an agent a 'conformist'; rather, such a specific designation of a person hinges upon his being seen as *especially* motivated to comply with otherwise routine requirements of situated conduct, or as noticeably preoccupied with or in some other way discernibly effortful in his satisfaction of routine requirements or normative contingencies.

Social categories of personhood provide the means whereby any particular person may be characterized, but this does not entail that 'personality' characteristics are themselves simply 'social roles'. Mischel argues that being a 'compassionate person' is not simply to be an incumbent of a social role; it is an attribute which is manifest in social roles, and can transcend particular roles, such as one individual's being a compassionate judge, a compassionate father, etc. He is especially adamant against what he sees to be a blurring of recognized distinctions between 'intimate' and 'social' relations, and between 'personal' and 'social' relations:

Normally, we speak of roles in connection with situations in which people treat each other as occupants of social positions; there are different socially defined patterns of expectations for London bobbies and New York cops. In this sense, there may be socially defined patterns of expectations for Victorian husbands and wives. But while any given husband and wife will have some patterns of expectations of each other, that pattern need not be role-structured and socially defined; indeed, one would normally say that the more personal their relation is, the less role-structured their expectations will be. All human relations, no matter what their specific character may be, depend on patterns of expectations people have of each other; but that is no reason to obliterate the distinction between relations which are social and those which are not social but personal.[7]

Mischel proceeds to acknowledge a distinction between the 'social' and the 'intersubjective', allowing the latter to capture what he has above termed the 'personal' relations of a husband and wife; thus, although a pattern of expectations between a husband and wife may not be 'social' as contrasted with 'personal' here, it *is* social in the sense of 'intersubjective'. However, Mischel proposes a further distinction:

Since we can say of someone that his personality at work is very different from what it is at home, there is a sense of 'self' in which the style in which a social role is performed can be called a 'presentation of self'. But there is another and quite different sense of 'self' in which we say that someone's personality shines through, or is expressed in, *everything he does* – in the different roles he performs and the way he performs them, as well as in the way he engages in those interpersonal relations that are not social roles . . . we can recognise the same personality at work in a variety of social and personal engagements because we can discern stylistic unities, character-istic of that person, *in all of his interpersonal engagements*.[8]

Although Mischel's remarks are cogent in confrontation with a particularly absorptive conception of 'role-enacting' behavior found in much interactionist literature, he too readily assumes the omni-relevance of personality in respect of 'everything' done, in relation to 'all . . . interpersonal engagements'. As noted, 'person-ality' assessments have their own 'occasionality' and require practical adequacy-criteria as well as normative or broadly evaluative-ethical ones. They cannot, either in principle or in practice, encompass *all* of an agent's conduct or modes of conduct, even as generalized descriptive assessments. There is no such transcendental vantage-point from which to make them. Mischel here overlooks the situatedly 'audienced' character of such attributions, their nature as differentially 'locally-purposeful' or 'theoretic' activities, as well as the grammatical constraints governing their scope and relevance. Further, the characterization of 'personality' as an attribute which 'shines through' is a metaphor suitable only for such 'personalities' as are positively esteemed. A major consideration which works to undermine the 'entification' of personality is this: most, if not all, designators of personality attributes consist in nominal compounds of adverbial qualifiers of conduct. The 'intelligent' person is one who does (some of) what he does intelligently; the 'fastidious' type is one who does (some of) what he does fastidiously; the 'bone-idle' is one who refrains from doing (much of) what he should do; the 'compassionate' person is one who engages in lines of activity which situatedly exhibit concern for the welfare of others, and so on. Not that such assessments are omni-relevantly undertaken even for occurrences (or repeated occurrences) of conduct 'potentially' so assessable. As

noted, any such assessments can be defeated by invoking occasioning aspects of situation or scene of conduct, relevantly prior
circumstances or prospects, and a motley of rule-ordered entitlements, justifications or excuses independent of an agent's claimed
'personal attributes'. As Burke long ago pointed out[9], characterolo-
gical inferences and ascriptions are but one set of a larger array of
resources for effecting explanations of actions or practices: other
'ratios' available for use include 'scene to act' (e.g., those housing
conditions would give anyone living there a lousy temper), 'purpose
to act' (e.g. if you want to get ahead, you have to make
compromises like that), 'act to act' (e.g. she's not usually charitable,
just owed him a favor), etc. Characteristics of 'personality' are,
then, in the first place and for the most part, properties assigned to
conduct along selectively evaluative dimensions. As Hogan, Jones
and Cheek remark in a recent overview,[10] '[a]lthough the total
number of trait words in English is quite large, present evidence
suggests they can be sorted or organised in terms of six broad
categories: These can be labelled intelligence, adjustment,
ambition, self-control, sociability and likeability.'[11] The nominali-
zation and projection of such attributable properties of public
performances to agents should not be confounded with the
detection of some state or stable feature intrinsic to an agent which
accords to his or her conduct the properties it is taken to have, no
matter how useful is such a device in courses of practical reasoning
and concerted activity.

Notes

1 Harold Garfinkel, *Studies in Ethnomethodology* (Prentice-Hall, N.J.,
   1967), p. 10, first advanced this proposal and specified its argumentative consequences for doing sociology.
2 Harvey Sacks et al., 'A Simplest Systematics for the Organization of
   Turn-Taking for Conversation'. In Jim Schenkein (ed.), *Studies in the
   Organization of Conversational Interaction* (Academic Press, N.Y.,
   1978), p. 43. 'With "recipient design" we intend to collect a multitude
   of respects in which the talk by a party in a[ny] conversation is
   constructed or designed in ways which display an orientation and
   sensitivity to the particular other(s) who are the co-participants. In
   our work, we have found recipient design to operate with regard to
   word selection, topic selection, the admissability and ordering of

sequences, the options and obligations for starting and terminating conversations and so on . . .'.

3   Cf. Lena Jayyusi, *Categorization and the Moral Order* (Routledge & Kegan Paul, London, 1984), chapter 1, 'Type categorizations'.

4   Charles D. Bolton, 'Is Sociology a Behavioral Science?'. In J.G. Manis and B.N. Meltzer (eds), *Symbolic Interaction* (Allyn & Bacon, Boston, 1967), p. 102.

5   Emanuel A. Schegloff, 'Between Micro and Macro: Contexts and Other Connections'. In Jeffrey C. Alexander et al. (eds), *The Micro-Macro Link* (University of California Press, Berkeley, 1987), p. 219. Cf. my 'Remarks on the Conceptualization of "Social Structure"', *Philosophy of the Social Sciences*, Vol. 12, No. 1, March 1982.

6   Jayyusi, *Categorization*, chapter 2, 'The social organization of categorial incumbency'.

7   Theodore Mischel, 'Conceptual Issues in the Psychology of the Self'. In his edited collection, *The Self: Psychological and Philosophical Issues* (Basil Blackwell, Oxford, 1977), p. 25.

8   Ibid., pp. 25–6, emphasis added.

9   Kenneth Burke, *A Grammar of Motives* (Prentice-Hall, N.J., 1945).

10   R. Hogan. W.H. Jones and J.M. Cheek, 'Socioanalytic Theory: An Alternative to Armadillo Psychology'. In Barry R. Schlenker (ed.), *The Self and Social Life* (McGraw-Hill, N.Y., 1985).

11   Ibid., p. 179. The authors base this factoring on the work of J.M. Digman and N.R. Takemoto-Chock, 'Factors in the Natural Language of Personality: Re-analysis, Comparison and Interpretation of Six Major Studies', *Multivariate Behavioral Research*, Vol. 16, 1981.

6

Realism and the Mind

First of all, we should be clear about the varieties of 'realism', some of which will not concern us here. Versions of that much caricatured philosophical position, 'naive realism', for example, according to which the ways we think about reality are (somehow) dictated to us by 'reality itself', are no longer of much interest to anyone: who wishes to appear 'naive'? More 'sophisticated' realisms abound, however, although even some of these uncomfortably teeter on the brink of naiveté: to whit, that form of 'realism' which insists on postulating that the world is what it is independently of our concepts of it and yet never gets around to specifying *independently of our concepts* in what it could possibly consist. Then there is that fellow-travelling 'realist' who, much impressed by the Sciences, speaks of 'Reality' as though it were a place like the Milky Way, ripe for penetration by the instruments and experiments of scientists, forgetting that, for example, physicists describe the way (certain) things are for the purposes of *physics* and not for the equally legitimate, non-comparable and therefore non-competitive, purposes of taxi-drivers, novelists and set-designers (to name but a threesome, with a truly realist professional heading the list).[1] And then there are the 'realists' of social science who, disaffected with Positivism (which, they claim, deals only with 'surface appearances' amenable to 'direct observation'), believe themselves privy to an 'underlying reality' of causal 'mechanisms' generating all of the purely surface effluvia we call, in our off-duty moments, everyday life.[2]

The kind of 'realism' which is sometimes invoked in arguments against the social-constructionist approach to knowledge is somewhat different from (albeit related to) these conceptions: it is a doctrine according to which true statements about states of affairs are made true by virtue of how things actually are 'objectively', *independently of how we may come to know of them.*[3] This is taken to *contrast* with social-constructionist ideas which are said to be based upon the claim that true statements are made true solely by virtue of a collective consensus to that effect and by no other, independent 'reference' to 'objective fact'. Indeed, the very category of 'objective fact' is held to be analysed or 'relativized' under the social-constructionist aegis into merely consensually corroborated and thus somehow artifactual 'posits' of one sort or another. 'Fact', 'objectivity' and the 'real' are spirited away, depicted as the upshots of merely 'rhetorical' accounting work linked to the protection or preservation of arbitrary authority, privilege or power relations within and among whichever social actors have recourse to them for practical purposes.

An initial reaction to positions such as these would be to query if any sense can be attached to the use of the concept 'independent' in a phrase like: 'independent reference to' the world or parts of it in such an argument. Independent of *what* social circumstance(s), of *which* method(s) of looking or telling, or of *which* person or collectivity? And in what could such putative 'independence' consist? A second quibble would be directed against the implicit assumption that, because situationally embedded, discursive practices of 'factual assertion', 'empirical demonstration', 'telling', 'giving accounts', 'arriving at judgements', 'describing what is to be seen, heard or felt', and so forth may be analysed into their constituent 'discursive devices', 'structures of practical rationality', 'aspects of recipient-design' and the rest, therefore no such discursively available rendition is available to a determination of its correctness, accuracy, truth or objectivity. The purely debunking use of the concept of 'rhetorical' in such an argument is insensitive to the varieties of functions of rhetoric itself, let alone the array of non-rhetorical but still discursive devices which characterize our practices of adducing truth-claims and ratifying them amongst each other.

I do not believe that there is a basis for any *generic* distinction between a healthy respect for ordinary uses of 'facticity' and 'objectivity' as canons of (successful) assessment on the one hand, and a commitment to 'social constructionism' on the other, as these are often counterposed.[4] Indeed, it is far from clear that 'social constructionism' is a philosophical *doctrine* of skepticism at all. Although some early variants of the 'labelling theory' of deviant conduct might be negatively so assessed, along with *some* formulations of Berger and Luckmann's 'thesis' of the social construction of 'reality', there are many proposals consonant with the theoretical objectives demarcated in these original positions which transcend a narrow dualism of 'objectivity' and 'social construction'. It seems plain enough that many things are socially constructed *to be* the objective, factual and 'real' phenomena (or versions of phenomena) that they are. One cannot systematically conflate how things are taken to be with how things are, although how things actually are cannot be wholly distinguished from how *discursive claims* about them are ratified or ratifiable.

Consider the date of my writing these words – 20 January 1988. This characterization of the date is wholly correct, objective and as factual as anything can be. And yet it is a wholly socio-historically constituted 'fact' in so far as (among other pertinent cultural considerations) it involves the deployment of the Gregorian calendar, which was adapted by Gregory Xlll from the Roman calendar as reformed by Julius Caesar in 45 BC. Gregory Xlll ordained that ten days be dropped in 1582 and years ending in hundreds be leap years only if divisible by 400: the Gregorian calendar was adopted in England in 1752, and is one among other possible calendars (the Judaic and Islamic calendars being the well-known alternatives, but the traditional Chinese calendar uses a very different metric. The French Revolutionary calendar, computed as from 22 September 1792 and deployed in France until 1805, furnishes another, albeit no longer used, variant). Note, moreover, that my *assertion about* the date in question stands as a factual *claim* whose social corroboration or defeat would only be consequential in virtue of normative limits of tolerance for errors in such a domain. If I turn out to be wrong by a day or two, then faulty watches, calendars or memories can be invoked: being wrong by weeks, months or years is *socially* much more serious! We invoke a plethora of 'mental' pathologies, from confusion to insanity, to handle such defects.

Relativity to socially constructed calendrical schemes, metrics of measurement, time zones, theoretical systems, legal systems, etc. in adducing factual or existential claims does not *undermine* their facticity or 'reality': for many issues, a simple dualism of 'relativity' versus 'realism' will not work. Where the vexed issues about 'objective', 'mind-independent' or intersubjectively-independent, 'facts of the matter' tend to arise most pointedly in connection with constructionist accounts is in the domain of the 'mental' and 'experiential'. For, as one typical argument goes, surely a person can entertain a wholly undisclosed thought unto death, having a certain clear content unknown to and unknowable to any other mortal being, and thus completely independent of any socially discernible conduct on his part? And if this much is possible, then surely we must acknowledge the additional possibility that anyone may, at any time, be enjoying a luxuriant 'inner mental life' without *any* intersubjective correlates, criteria or methods of attributional detection coming into play? Surely, we must recognise a distinction between something's actually *being* thus-and-so and our *knowing that* it is thus-and-so?

In the philosophy of mathematics, a similar issue crops up in connection with the dispute between those 'constructivists' who seek to abandon the Law of Excluded Middle, which asserts that, for any mathematical proposition, either it is correct or it is incorrect *independent* of anyone's actual determination, and those who seek to maintain it. Those who wish to abandon it argue that, prior to the construction of a proof, there can be no sense accorded to the assertion that there 'exists' a determinate answer to a mathematical conjecture, whilst those who wish to maintain it argue that by proving a mathematical conjecture one essentially 'discovers' the correct answer which was already there waiting to be demonstrated: the proof does not merely 'construct' a correct answer – it 'reveals' it.[5] The transition from conjecture to theorem consequent upon adducing a proof is held to be a matter of arriving at a determination *which was there to be arrived at*. It is a revelation of an 'abstract (mathematical) object', in Platonistic terms. It is in this sense especially that many have discerned an affinity between topics in the philosophy of mind and in the philosophy of mathematics, especially those topics informed by Wittgenstein's contributions to both. For one aspect of the picture of the mind against which Wittgenstein and his successors strenuously argued involved the notion that determining someone's mental occurrence(s), state(s) or orientations could be construed as a matter of revealing some hidden but 'real' phenomena, different from physical phenomena only by virtue of their ethereal, spiritual or 'abstract' properties. Discovering and disclosing correctly something about someone's mental state is, according to the conception Wittgenstein was concerned to combat, closely analogous to discovering and disclosing correctly some hidden *phenomenon*. For some such phenomena, however, their 'existence' may be posited quite independently of any particular methods of discovery.

I cannot here enter into the details of the disputes between constructivists and Platonists, intuitionists and formalists in the philosophy of mathematics,[6] but propose instead to focus upon the central issue, that of the putative disconnectability of 'fact' from method of determination, in the domain of cognition and social action. *I shall be arguing that no generic being/knowing or ontic/ epistemic distinction can be sustained in the domain of the 'mental'.* This claim for a generic distinction will be referred to here as the 'determination-independence argument'. My position may be termed an '*anti*-independence' argument. (I shall not go into any details about the relationship of the 'determination-independence' argument to Platonistic philosophy of mathematics and its related insistence upon the generic applicability of the Law of Excluded Middle in this discussion, but some of the inspiration for my position here derives from the debate generated by that proposal.) I shall then attempt to demonstrate the relevance of its demise for the social-constructionist approach to the characterization of the mental.

There are several threads to this argument. The first concerns what I shall term the role of the putatively 'transcendental witness' in 'thought-experiments' (*Gedanken*experiments) of the kind designed to permit the 'demonstration-independence' argument; the second consideration is that of the fallacy of reification or 'misplaced concreteness' in the domain of the mental, and, finally, I shall try to show, with reference to the case of hypnosis and 'hypnotic trance', that the de-reifying, constructionist viewpoint does not entail any claim to the effect that ascriptions of mental predicates are merely 'rhetorical devices', and that 'mental states' are somehow 'unreal', but rather that their characteristics have systematically been mystified. The result should be not so much a 'reconciliation' of 'realism' with 'social constructionism' construed as 'doctrines' or 'philosphical theories', but a realization of the sociohistorically constituted character of our determinations of the nature of the mind and the mental.

The Transcendental Witness

Let us survey the following claims:

1 'She thought often of her dead mother, but never told anyone.'
2 'He sneered inwardly as they spoke, but sustained a lively and deceptive appearance of comradeship throughout the encounter.'
3 'No one else was ever inducted into their secret covenant, a private bond which died with them on the battlefield.'
4 'He could make it appear, convincingly, that he was recollecting a real event, but only he knew that he was describing the content of the same, recurring dream.'
5 'Only he could know the depths of his despair.'

Such attributions are the very stuff from which generic being/knowing dichotomies are forged in this domain. How is the truth-value of such reports to be assessed? Surely, not by appeal to public avowal or conduct in context(s), since in each case the 'mental' state, event or series of states or events is characterized as wholly unavailable to anyone except for their 'possessor' (excluding no. 3, which does not concern anything 'mental', and to which we shall return). What is to be made of this? One argument postulates the *invariant or generic privacy* of the mental on the basis of cases such as these, but we have said enough already about this Cartesian misconception; no shared, intelligible concepts of the mental could arise for linguistic usage of any sort, including the formulation of descriptions such as the above, were such a generic thesis to be true. However, such cases do fuel the fires of a peculiar but stubborn kind of 'mental realism': the contingently undisclosed 'mental' state, event or orientation is held to be a *phenomenon* available only to an inner sense, and its existence can be vouchsafed independently of *any* public context of disclosure. Indeed, *every* public sign available can be systematically at variance with the 'true' or 'real' state of mind of the individual concerned. The attributions listed in the above passages 1–5 seem to count as determination-independent revelations of possibly true and real 'underlying' states of affairs.

Enter, now, the skeptic. How could the reporter of the above states of affairs possibly *know* them to be (or to have been) existing, as distinct from surmising or stipulating their existence, especially those which are set up as states of affairs *never* revealed to *anyone, including the narrator*? Why should anyone 'believe' them? Well, we can look to our own lives for principled corroboration of their *possible* truth: haven't we often successfully concealed thoughts, attitudes and emotions from others who never did find out about our concealments? Something that may *possibly* be true may *actually* be true for some *particular instance*: why not these instances? In any case, these are literary or literary-historical passages – their usefulness here is to argue for the principled possibility that such could be actual descriptions of actual states of affairs. But, then, who would or could proffer such descriptions, when and on what grounds, *literary licence apart*? Are we in a similar predicament to that of Hunter's private conversationalists in the following scenario?

a conversation at which no one was present but myself and my dying friend. We say he was dying in order to eliminate any later testimony of his as to the course of the conversation; and to eliminate 'relational clues' we will suppose that he was somewhat delirious, did not reminisce about his past or mention his family or friends, spoke in a way very uncharacteristic of his normal personality, and directed me to a buried treasure which on no interpretation of his instructions was discoverable . . . while no one could have any grounds for *affirming* that I got any of it [the conversation] right, it is monstrous to say that the question whether I got any of it right makes no sense – if this implies, as I think it does, that 'I don't know whether to believe him or not'.[7]

To this, Hunter remarks, someone might respond that we know what it *would be like* to verify the report even if, in fact, we cannot practically do so. There *could*, after all, have been a witness. Yet one cannot know what to make 'of the idea of someone else being present at a conversation at which no one else was present.'[8] This is a clear counterpart to my third passage above, but it has a natural extension to the other cases in which, not secret or private interpersonal encounters are at issue, but the 'hidden' thoughts, dreams or attitudes (etc.) of particular individuals.

I shall refer to this predicament as involving the peculiar status of a 'Transcendental Witness'. This Witness can make attributions in the *absence* of the ordinary sorts of ascription conditions. They are set up as method-of-determination-independent. Such a privilege marks out any such reporter or witness *as* Transcendental. In accepting the possible correctness or, minimally, the plausibility, of what is characterized as a private, 'mental' state of affairs (for the purposes of narrative construction or plot advancement or whatever) we are indulging in an occasioned *suspension* of the kind of skeptical questioning just alluded to.

Can I sneer inwardly while deceiving my company into believing (falsely) of me that I am enjoying myself? Can I harbor a private thought and never disclose its contents to a living soul? Can I portray what I secretly know to be a dream as a vivid recollection and get away with it? Can I endure a profound mental anguish which is revealed to no one else? Of course, all of these things are possible, but only under certain kinds of circumstances, and *their occurrence does not involve my observation or knowledge of some 'real, underlying mental phenomenon' susceptible of 'revelation' to myself.* The contingent 'privacy' of my undisplayed attitude, concealed thought, disguised dream-recollection and hidden mental anguish does not consist in my having 'inner access' to such things in the manner of a witness to a scene or an observer of an object. This much we sought to establish in chapter 4. However, the possibility of insincerity in any given instance may be mistakenly linked to an assumption that it 'betokens the necessity of knowledge',[9] so that the assertion that one has been insincere in one's disclosure, performance or conduct in a case involving thoughts, attitudes or emotions may be thought to entail 'private knowledge' of the 'real' or 'true' 'underlying' state of affairs. When I lie, in words or deeds, about my thoughts and feelings, then do I *know* or am I conscious

that I am really thinking or feeling thus-and-so and not as I said [or did]? This is wrong, for the very phrase 'to know that I am lying' is misleading. One may find out that one has unintentionally been deceiving someone, but one does not *find out* that one is lying .... The inner voice of guilt presupposes the lie and does not 'inform' me of it.[10]

To mislead others about my thoughts, attitudes or emotions is not to *know* what I think or feel and to say/do something different; it is to think X and say/do otherwise or to feel thus-and-so and to deny it in words and/or deeds.[11] If one cannot, logically, be said to 'find out that', to 'learn that', or to 'realize that' one thinks or feels X or Y, nor to 'misidentify' or be 'mistaken about' (as distinct from *untruthful* about) one's thoughts or feelings, then one cannot be said to *know* such things, either. We *do* say things like: 'I don't know what I think (want, feel)', but, as Hacker reminds us, 'none of these concern *ignorance*'[12]. When I say that I don't know what I think or feel about such-and-such, I am not saying that I need to find out more about what is going on inside my head (except in a clearly metaphorical sense); but that I have not yet formulated an opinion or decided what I want or how I feel. For instance, if I say: 'I was thinking it is a nice day for a picnic', to use an example of Hunter's, 'I am not saying I am not quite sure yet whether it is a nice day for a picnic, I will need to check further, but that I do not take the fact that it is a nice day as settling what we should do.'[13] Deciding upon such matters is nothing remotely like searching for a hidden phenomenon which, once uncovered, becomes an object of knowledge; nor is one about to embark upon a process of interior checking or 'monitoring' the results of 'inner processes' in cases of tentativeness about what one thinks or feels.

Reification and 'Neuralization' of the Mental

If we consider a wider range of cases of the 'mental' life, we shall see how far-fetched it is to suppose that the elements of the mental domain are purely internally discoverable matters for individuals, such that an issue concerning their putatively 'independent' status might even be raised. Consider 'understanding', 'remembering', 'recollecting' ('recalling', etc.), 'perceiving', 'knowing', 'realizing' and sundry other cognate 'mental' verbs. These are all *defeasible-achievement* concepts (Ryle), presupposing the *demonstrable facticity or accuracy* of what it is one is claiming to have understood, remembered, seen, realized, etc. Such concepts do not name discrete states, events or 'phenomena' susceptible to first-person 'revelation', 'observation' or 'internal monitoring' of any kind. Claims to facticity are dismissable, defeasible, by public recourse to convincingly established counter-evidences of all sorts. Thus, a purely individual and non-demonstrable claim made privately to oneself about such matters *cannot be sufficient to assure that*, indeed, one *has* understood, remembered, perceived, known, realized, etc., whatever it is that one says (to oneself) one has understood, remembered (etc.), *as distinct from merely thinking that one has understood, remembered, seen* what it is that one *claims*. We argued in chapter 3 against the intelligibility of 'subjective sovereignty' in respect of comprehension, rule-following and the justification of a variety of 'mental' and experiential claims: the notion of 'independently-existing' inner or 'mental' phenomena applied here simply trades upon the theme of individual, subjective sovereignty, as well as the reification of the mental predicates. Among the many thinkers who fail to come to terms with these arguments is John Searle, who maintains, stipulatively, that: 'Some mental concepts, such as, for example, *having a pain* or *believing* that so and so, denote *entities* that *exist* entirely in the mind . . . . We cannot define mental *phenomena* in terms of their behavioral manifestations, because we know that it is *always* possible to *have the phenomena* independently of having *any* behavioral manifestations.'[14] Note the clear reification or 'entification' of pains and beliefs and their projection into the 'mind'; not only are pains and beliefs not 'entities' at all, it is strikingly inappropriate to claim that all pains 'exist in the mind' – that is precisely the sort of thing one might say to someone about whose complaints of pain one had reason for being suspicious! In a discussion of the concept of 'belief', Hunter assails recurrent misconceptions in which it is depicted as a 'state' (whether mental or neural in kind), misconceptions especially rife among proponents of computationalist psychology and even among some of its critics:

If there were a computer that was designed to evaluate evidence and arguments and always deliver a verdict, but to mark verdicts 'beliefs' when the evidence or arguments were inconclusive, then although we, having designed the thing, might know all about what state it was in when it marked a verdict a belief, we would still not take it to be *saying* that it was in that state, but rather that the answer it gave was to be preferred, although there was room for doubt. If it was further designed to explain why it marked anything a belief, it would not avert to the state it was in but, for example, to the fact that such and such evidence was missing or to the other explanations of the facts at its disposal which were just possible. Even if the machine were designed in such a way that on detecting a certain state of itself, it marked a verdict a belief, it would not be talking about itself, but about the verdict, in so marking it.'[15]

Note as well the persistent tendency to think of the functioning of mental predicates as names for inner 'phenomena' wholly and invariantly detachable from conduct and and – which Searle completely neglects – the relevant ascription *contexts* of conduct. This is the stuff that myths are made of: it is not 'social constructionism' but misguided efforts to mimic the physical sciences that obstruct a clear view of the nature of the mental in man.

Neural states and processes of various kinds may well be implicated in the factors which enable us to feel pain and to entertain the beliefs that we do, but it is a source of confusion to attempt to identify the experience of pain or the espousal of a belief with neural conditions of any sort, or to reduce the former to the latter. Such is Searle's persistent inclination. Departing somewhat from earlier efforts to effect a 'theoretical identity' between the 'mental' and the 'neural', such as the Place–Smart materialist account according to which brain states/processes are mental states/processes by analogy to the 'identity' of water droplet clusters with clouds, or water with H_2O,[16] Searle none the less seeks to locate various 'experiential phenomena' in the brain:

But where, then, is the visual experience . . .? It is right there in the brain where these [causal] processes have been going on. That is, the visual experience is caused by the functioning of the brain in response to external optical stimulation of the visual system, but it is also realised in the structure of the brain. A story similar in form, though quite different in content, can be told about thirst . . . . On such an account, thirst is caused by neural events in the hypothalamus and realised in the hypothalamus. It doesn't matter for our purposes if this account is actually the correct account of thirst, the point is that it is a possible account.[17]

Accordingly, 'if one knew the principles on which the brain worked one could infer that it was in a state of thirst or having a visual experience.'[18] But could it make sense to claim that *my brain* is thirsty, rather than myself? Hypothalamic events may well (co-) generate experience(s) characteristic of thirst in my throat, my stomach, head etc., but it is at best a poor joke to propose that it is my brain that requires a glass of water to assuage *its* thirst. Or perhaps some philosophers simply lack a sense of humor. Moreover, the notion of localizing a 'visual experience' as well as the very concept of a 'visual experience' are problematic in several respects in this connection. As I look around me, trying to find out who just entered my room, I certainly *see* various things, but it is an abuse of the expression 'to have an experience' to call such a state of affairs as my seeing things as I am looking around one of 'having a visual experience'. We reserve this expression for special circumstances, such as, *inter alia*, being especially struck by a beautiful sunset or by being absorbed in the appreciation of a wonderful painting. In those cases in which we may genuinely avow, or be described as, having a visual experience, the content of that experience as depictable could hardly consist in neuronal firing patterns. Not only are such phenomena rarely objects of vision at all, they are certainly not what I could mundanely describe when I describe a visual experience of the kind just mentioned. If it is argued that such firings *facilitate* my experiences, all well and good, but the visual experiences which they facilitate are not themselves in my brain – they aren't anywhere! What they are experiences *of* (e.g. the sunset or the painting) have locations, but it makes no sense to say: 'Fine, so that's where the objects of your experience are located, but now tell me where your experiences of those objects are located.' To attempt to give this nonsensical question an 'answer' would betoken a failure to note that the use of the verb 'having' has multiple functions and is not restricted to *one* use, that of signalling 'possession'. 'Having money' may presuppose a location, but 'having obligations' doesn't. Neither does 'having a visual experience'. Again, we encounter a common, but false, assumption that a commonality of (surface-)grammatical form among varieties of expressions entails a singular pattern of application in usage. Searle, and many others, consistently overlook this fact in their haste to relate the phenomena of 'mind' and 'experience' exclusively to neurophysiological inquiry.[19]

If 'understanding', 'perceiving', 'remembering', 'believing', 'having an experience' (etc.) are not logically identical to, or reducible to, neural phenomena, what of the more esoterically subjective or 'mental' states such as 'hypnotic trance'? Surely *there* we shall find a pure case of a mode of experiencing that is amenable to psychologistic 'realism' and ripe for neural reduction?

Hypnotic Trance: A Special Subjective State?

'Mesmerism' (after Mesmer, whose original interest in 'trance states' lies at the origins of hypnosis and hypnotic phenomena as topics of scientific interest) has metamorphosed considerably over two hundred years. Mesmer's own explanation for the phenomena of what later became known as 'hypnosis', namely, a kind of 'animal' magnetism, fell foul of the Franklin Commission which was established to inquire into such claims. However, the Commission, having concluded that Mesmer's *explanation* was unacceptable, concluded rashly that the *phenomena* for which it was put forward were also discredited.

De Puysegur is accredited with having discovered 'artificial' or 'magnetic' somnambulism in 1782, and James Braid first claimed to have witnessed two demonstrations of this in 1841, subsequently recategorizing the phenomena 'hypnotism', or 'nervous sleep'. Liebeault and Bernheim later transformed Braid's conception of hypnotism as an all-or-nothing 'state' involving the appearance of sleep to one in which 'suggestion' played a considerable part: it turned out that de Puysegur's somnambulists made up less than one per cent of all individuals undergoing hypnotic induction procedures, and a picture of an 'active subject' slowly took the place of the classical portrayal of a passive, 'weak-willed' recipient of the hypnotist's operations.[20] Much contemporary physiological research corroborates the claim about the mental 'activity' of the hyponotized subject,[21] and even Charcot believed that hypnotizability depended far more upon the suggestibility of a subject – viz. his or her willingness and preparedness to submit to and entertain the proposals for experience and action furnished by the clinician hypnotist – than upon the hypnotist's own 'charisma', 'powers' or contributions to the induction procedure.[22]

In this century, a serious transformation has occurred in the thinking of those who make hypnotic phenomena their professional subject of study. Among the most prominent of the 'anti-special-state' theorists has been Theodore X. Barber.[23] Barber, and a growing number of colleagues and students, conducted a wide range of studies and proposed a 'social-psychological' shift in our conception of hypnosis, away from a 'realism' of 'trance states' and toward a characterization of the phenomena formerly subsumed under 'trance' as *strategic forms of social action.*[24]

Even those espousing a 'special-state' theory of hypnotic phenomena, such as Orne[25] and Hilgard,[26] employ concepts deriving from interactionist social psychology in formulating their positions,[27] and virtually no one in the field any longer maintains that subjects lose control and fall 'under the power' of a hypnotizing clinician.[28] Indeed, as Edmonston remarks, the study area is often defined as encompassing 'the phenomena of social suggestibility, not hypnosis as conceived by the originator of the term'.[29]

In many cases, an hypnotic-induction procedure consists in a sequence of instructions/suggestions to the subject that he or she physically relax and attempt to engage the imagination in a series of tasks which can facilitate the goal of the hypnosis. One of Barber's most interesting procedures involved persuading compliant subjects to imagine, as vividly as possible, that their hand, about to be inserted into freezing water, was an icicle about to plunge into refreshingly ice-blue whirling eddies wherein it would swirl about dissolving in a chilling blast.[30] Only the most sustained, effortful, collaborative imaginative activity could engender the temporary analgesia which such an image can afford. Of course, this is an 'altered state of awareness', but not in any radically esoteric sense. As Wagstaff remarks:

Perhaps all that can really be concluded is that whilst it may be inaccurate to say that 'hypnosis' is *an* altered state of consciousness, it may be logically consistent to say the phenomena that have been labelled as 'hypnotic' may be accompanied by altered *states* of consciousness, *if* we include altered states of consciousness which accompany obedience, compliance, relaxation and concentration.[31]

People may differ somewhat in terms of their willingness and capacity to engage in the sort of active fantasizing, concentration, focal attention and general cooperativeness required for 'successful' hypnotic performance, as well as in their preparedness to adopt interpretive schemes particular to the 'lore' of hypnotism for the post-hypnosis conceptualization of their experiences and responses (e.g. as having been 'involuntary', as having been 'out of awareness', etc.).[32] None the less, a central claim defended in much current work in this field is that an 'hypnotic state' is a not a discrete mental phenomenon of an esoteric kind induced solely by esoteric procedures of interpersonal control, but consists rather in diverse processes of actively collaborative imagining (generating vivid images suggested to the subject), concentrating focally upon them, orienting to suggestions as instructions which should be followed, performing on cue, etc., all of which are to be found in various combinations in other, widely diverse areas of ordinary living. The police officer who suggests to the witness that he attempt to relax and try hard to recall the face of the assailant, the dentist who proposes that a palate injection will feel like a 'little bee-sting', the teacher who encourages compliance in timed responses from a student, all participate in various ways and to varying degrees of intensity in the phenomena grouped under 'hypnotic induction'.

In concluding his recent, extensive overview of the field, encompassing putative forms of 'hypnotic' blindness, age regression, analgesia, amnesia and hallucination, Wagstaff concludes:

the set of historical accidents, or the 'comedy of errors' which gave rise to modern concepts of hypnosis has also produced some interesting beneficent consequences. In playing this 'game' of hypnosis along the way both hypnotists and subjects have also chanced upon examples of the benefits of relaxation in the removal of anxiety and pain, covert conditioning in the treatment of maladaptive behaviors, and the importance of patient-therapist interaction.'[33]

The demystification of 'hypnosis' and its empirical treatment as a social process does not result in its *disappearance* as a phenomenon, but rather its decomposition into varieties of interpersonal, compliance-induction and acceptance forms employing discursive strategies and conceptual schemes of analysable kinds.

Concluding Remarks

The forms of availability of the 'mental' are enormously diverse, and the possibilities of concealment of various 'mental' and 'experiential' states and processes sometimes engenders a spurious pan-skepticism concerning our capacities to ascertain the mental/experiential situations of others. Moreover, the individual 'locus' for ascriptions and avowals of mental predicates (from 'X believes that Y' to 'X is hypnotized') can mislead us into thinking of the 'mental' as consisting entirely in subjective, internal, discrete 'phenomena'. When confronted with arguments which seek to reassert the conceptual and pragmatic connections between mental and experiential states of affairs and observable, public, social conduct, contexts, conceptual schemata and their grammars, some hasten to resurrect a metaphysics of 'mental realism', trying to 'relocate' the loci for, or 'referents' of, the mental predicates entirely inside persons' heads (minds or brains). In response to counter-arguments inspired by Wittgenstein and others, proponents of mental realism invoke one or another 'determination-independence' argument.

They claim that constructionist analysts seek theoretically to *replace* the so-called 'inner' reality of mind (which, according to some, is 'ultimately' an inner reality of neural phenomena alone) with talk of merely peripheral matters such as what people say and do in various circumstances using various discursive devices and schemata.

In this discussion, I have tried to track down some of the consequences of these 'realist' proposals in an effort to show (i) that the general assumption of determination-independence in the domain of the mental, i.e. that one can know what it is like for a mental-predicate ascription to be true without *anyone* being able to know it (cf. Stolzenberg),[34] is, at best, a shaky proposition; (ii) that various forms of 'realism' in cognitive studies result in committing the fallacy of misplaced concreteness or reification; (iii) that some forms of reification underlie contemporary forms of mind/brain identity theorizing; and (iv) that constructionist accounts of various mental states (such as hypnotic 'trance' states), while they may contribute to debunking excessive claims made about the phenomena, do not simply result in the wholesale dissolution of the phenomena but rather in their properly socio-logical apprehension.

Notes

1   These remarks are touched off by a reading of J.L. Austin's strictures about the 'real' and 'reality' in his *Sense and Sensibilia* (Clarendon Press, Oxford, 1962) and Gilbert Ryle's oft-neglected warnings against dichotomizing the 'worlds' of 'Science' and of everyday life in his *Dilemmas* (Cambridge University Press, Cambridge, 1954).

2   Cf. A. Sayer, *Method in Social Science: A Realist Approach* (Hutchinson, London, 1984); R.W. Outhwaite, 'Toward a Realist Perspective'. In G. Morgan (ed.), *Beyond Method* (Sage, Berkeley, California, 1983); R. Bhaskar, *A Realist Theory of Science* (Harvester Press, Brighton, 1978, 2nd edn); and his *The Possibility of Naturalism* (Harvester Press, Brighton, 1979); and R. Keat and J. Urry, *Social Theory as Science* (Routledge & Kegan Paul, London, 1975).

3   See, for example, Michael Dummett, 'Realism'. In his *Truth and Other Enigmas* (Duckworth, London, 1978).

4   Such a counterposition is perhaps more evident among the constructionists in social psychology than elsewhere. See, for example, Ken Gergen's introduction to Kenneth Gergen and Keith Davis (eds.), *The*

Social Construction of the Person (Springer International, N.Y., 1985).

5 For some illuminating discussion of this issue, see Gabriel Stolzenberg's paper, 'Can an Inquiry into the Foundations of Mathematics tell us Anything about Mind?'. In Paul Watzlawick (ed.), *The Invented Reality* (Norton, N.Y., 1984).

6 For a useful compendium, see Paul Benacerraf and Hilary Putnam's edited selection, *Philosophy of Mathematics* (Cambridge University Press, Cambridge, 2nd edition, 1983). For a lively Wittgensteinian commentary on these issues, see S.G. Shanker, *Wittgenstein and the Turning-Point in the Philosophy of Mathematics* (State University of New York Press, N.Y., 1987), especially chapter 8.

7 J.F.M. Hunter, 'Some Questions About Dreaming'. In his *Essays After Wittgenstein* (University of Toronto Press, 1973), p. 76.

8 Ibid.

9 Hacker, *Insight and Illusion*, p. 300.

10 Ibid.

11 Ibid. Hacker does not address himself to the specific issue of *non-discursive* and misleading/deceptive displays of thoughts, feelings, etc., but the point can, I think, be extended to encompass them.

12 Ibid., p. 302.

13 J.F.M. Hunter, 'Wittgenstein and Materialism', *Mind*, Vol. 86, No. 344, October 1977, p. 521.

14 John Searle, 'Mind and Brains Without Programs'. In Colin Blakemore and Susan Greenfield (eds), *Mindwaves: Thoughts on Intelligence, Identity and Consciousness* (Basil Blackwell, 1987), pp. 229–31, emphasis added.

15 J.F.M. Hunter, 'Believing'. In Peter A. French et al. (eds), *Midwest Studies in Philosophy Volume V: Studies in Epistemology* (University of Minnesota Press, Minneapolis, 1980), p. 248.

16 For some discussion of these theses, see the collection edited by C.V. Borst, *The Mind/Brain Identity Theory* (Macmillan, N.Y., 1970); and for an assessment, particularly in regard to 'thoughts' and 'recognition', see my 'The Brain as Agent', *Human Studies*, Vol. 2, No. 4, October 1979. For a fuller elaboration of the relationship between postulated neural phenomena and the achievement of 'recognition' in human beings, see my ' "Recognition" in Wittgenstein and Contemporary Thought'. In M. Chapman and R. Dixon (eds), *Meaning and the Growth of Understanding: Wittgenstein's Significance for Developmental Psychology* (Springer International, N.Y., 1986).

17 John Searle, *Intentionality: An Essay in the Philosophy of Mind* (Cambridge University Press, Cambridge, 1983), p. 267.

18 Ibid., p. 268.

19 Searle, in Blakemore and Greenfield (eds), *Mindwaves*, p. 231, on the 'principle of neurophysiological sufficiency'.

20 For a fuller account, see the contributions of Bond and Weitzenhoffer in David Waxman et al. (eds), *Modern Trends in Hypnosis* (Plenum Press, N.Y., 1985).

21 E.g. F.G. McGuigan, *Cognitive Psychophysiology* (Erlbaum, N.J., 1978).

22 See 'The Debates over Hypnotism'. In Frank J. Sulloway's classic work, *Freud: Biologist of the Mind* (Basic Books, N.Y., 1983), pp. 42–9. Sulloway remarks that, by 1893, the work of Bernheim and others 'had succeeded in convincing Freud that much of Charcot's evidence for the physiological nature of hypnosis was completely bogus' (p. 49).

23 I am most grateful to Professor Barber for permitting me to visit him and his team at Medfield Hospital, Massachusetts, to discuss these issues. Much of what I argue here is inspired by his pioneering researches.

24 See, *inter alia*, T.X. Barber, *Hypnosis: A Scientific Approach* (Van Nostrand Reinhold, N.Y., 1969); T.X. Barber et al., *Hypnotism, Imagination and Human Potentialities* (Pergamon Press, N.Y., 1974); Graham F. Wagstaff, *Hypnosis, Compliance and Belief* (St Martin's Press, N.Y., 1981); and Nicholas P. Spanos, 'Hypnotic Behavior: A Social-Psychological Interpretation of Amnesia, Analgesia and "Trance Logic"', *The Behavioral and Brain Sciences*, Vol. 9, 1986. This paper generated 22 peer commentaries and a concluding summary by Spanos.

25 M.T. Orne, 'The Nature of Hypnosis: Artifact and Essence', *Journal of Abnormal and Social Psychology*, Vol. 58, 1959 and his 'Hypnosis, Motivation and Compliance', *American Journal of Psychiatry*, Vol. 122, 1966.

26 E.R. Hilgard, *Divided Consciousness* (Wiley, N.Y., 1977). In this text, Hilgard advanced an influential theory of hypnotic phenomena often referred to as 'neo-dissociationism'. According to Hilgard, hypnotized subjects lose conscious control over their conduct; such control is effectively relinquished to dissociated cognitive 'subsystems' operating behind amnesic barriers.

27 See Richard St. Jean, 'Hypnosis: Artichoke or Onion?', *Behavioral and Brain Sciences*, Vol. 9, 1986, p. 482.

28 See Patricia G. Bowers, 'Understanding Reports of Nonvolition', *Behavioral and Brains Sciences*, p. 469. See also Peter L.N. Naish's comment: 'nearly all currently active researchers would endorse the Spanos position' (p. 476). Spanos's position is essentially a development of Barber's views, and he worked collaboratively with Barber for several years.

29 William E. Edmonston Jr, 'Hypnosis and Social Suggestibility'. In ibid., p. 471. Not that Edmonston welcomes this development: for him, 'we must return to basics and study, not the social suggestibility, but the historically defined condition of hypnosis and its spontaneous – unsuggested – phenomena. Braid's original definition of hypnotism and its fundamental characteristic, relaxation, need to be the focus of our investigations'. (p. 471)

30 Personal communication, Dr T.X. Barber.

31 Wagstaff, *Hypnosis, Compliance and Belief*, p. 214.

32 For fuller discussion of these claims made by some subjects, see N.P. Spanos, 'More on the Social Psychology of Hypnotic Responding', *Behavioral and Brain Sciences*, Vol. 9, No. 3, 1986, pp. 489–93.

33 Wagstaff, *Hypnosis*, p. 220.

34 Stolzenberg, 'Can an Inquiry . . .?, p. 302.

7

Explanation, Psychologism and Social Construction

The idea that what people do is ultimately to be explained with reference to their 'psychological states and processes' or, more currently, in terms of their 'cognitive' or 'information-processing' capacities, is deeply appealing to contemporary culture. We live in the age of the computer. We have not fully emancipated ourselves from the ideologies of atomistic individualism and psychologisms of various kinds, both in our everyday 'theorizing' and in the behavioral sciences. We are still, in significant measure, even after Wittgenstein, the intellectual heirs to Descartes. We are informed, with due deference to evolutionary fact and theory, that we are, after all, merely higher forms of animals – 'organisms' – or, more fashionably, in the era of Artificial Intelligence, 'species' of 'information-processing systems'. As such, we belong, in our totality, to the causal order governing natural or mechanical phenomena. Any insistence to the contrary is liable to be treated as a mark of regression to theological precepts or, worse, to anti-intellectual 'irrationalism', in various quarters.

An integral feature of this contemporary intellectual scene is the insistence upon the general propriety of *some* kind of causal account of rational, human conduct. In this final chapter, I want to oppose some widely influential but, I believe, wholly mistaken defenses of this view. One of my purposes is to show that any inclinations to label anti-causalist accounts of (the bulk of) human conduct as non- or anti-scientific are misplaced. I shall begin by discussing the contribution of Donald Davidson in his classic paper, 'Actions, Reasons and Causes'.[1] Subsequently, I shall take up the theme that 'reason-giving' is itself an investigable form of conventionalized social praxis, alongside the arrays of situated actions by which it is occasioned, and that its sociological elucidation as such constitutes an analysis of a commonplace kind of 'cognitive' conduct.

'Beliefs', 'Desires' and Primary Reasons

Davidson states his theses about causality and human action-explanation succinctly, and then seeks to defend them against anticipated rebuttals. The best way to proceed, then, is to trace his steps methodically and see to what extent his position is defensible. He starts out articulating two fundamental claims:

Giving the reason why an agent did something is often a matter of naming the pro attitude (a) or the related belief (b) or both; let me call this pair the *primary reason* why the agent performed the action. Now it is possible to reformulate the claim that rationalisations are causal explanations, and give structure to the argument as well, by stating two theses about primary reasons:

1.   For us to understand how a reason of any kind rationalises an action it is necessary and sufficient that we see, at least in essential outline, how to construct a primary reason.
2.   The primary reason for an action is its cause.[2]

Further specifying his concept of a 'primary reason', Davidson proposes that: '*R* is a primary reason why an agent performed the action *A* under the description *d* only if *R* consists of a 'pro attitude' of the agent toward actions with a certain property, and a belief of the agent that *A*, under the description *d*, has that property.'[3] Davidson makes this particularisation in order to accommodate the fact that reasons explain (Davidson says: 'rationalize' here) what someone does only when the action in question 'is described in one way and not in another'[4].

Throughout his argument, Davidson most unfortunately uses the terms 'rationalizes/rationalization' as synonymous with 'explains/explanation'. In ordinary usage, to say of someone that his reason-as-given amounts to a 'rationalization' can often, if not invariably, be a way of characterizing his reason-as-given as designed to show him in the best possible light, as a 'mere' piece of *post hocery* and, consequently, as somewhat less than (perhaps even not in the least) an *explanation* of why he acted as he did.

Matters are made worse when Davidson posits rationalizations as 'a species of causal explanation'.[5] Granting, for the moment, the infelicitous identity between 'reason', 'explanation' and 'rationalization' in Davidson's account, let us probe the heart of the argument. It is, essentially, this:

> Central to the relation between a reason and an action it explains is the idea that the agent performed the action *because* he had the reason. Of course, we can include this idea too in justification; but then the notion of justification becomes as dark as the notion of reason until we can account for the force of that 'because'.[6]

Davidson urges, against Melden and other logicians of action following Wittgenstein, that if we restrict ourselves to specifying patterns, contexts and conventions of activities in adducing the reasons agents have for them, rendering talk of causes irrelevant, 'then we are without an analysis of the "because" in "He did it because . . .", where we go on to name a reason.'[7]

I think that one point emerges here: an unnoticed proclivity on Davidson's part to treat 'has a reason' as exhaustively either: 'is justified (by)', where one imputes (rational) grounds to the agent which he may (or may not) have considered or to which he may not himself assent, or: 'possesses a reason R' in some sense analogous to the occurrence of a causally effective event or state. Since we are told that the former sense is not yet akin to that of a 'primary reason' (since one can, accordingly, 'have' a reason and not act, or 'be justified in Xing' and not X), then we are left with the latter which, alone, qualifies as properly causal. The allegedly *causal* property of this putatively 'primary' sense of 'having a reason' is held to explain the force of 'because' in constructions such as: 'He did X because . . .' where we are correct in stating *his* reason rather than just *a* (perhaps excellent) reason for his action.

However, the force of 'because' in such locutions is far from uniform, and extremely rarely is it properly causal. To give just two alternative options, commonly realized, I may claim to have done something because X, where X may state a purpose to be realised (e.g. 'I wanted to get rich') or a convention or rule to be followed (e.g. 'The light was red'). Purposes are not antecedents, and rules and conventions are neither events nor states 'owned' by those conforming to them. Neither have the qualifications to operate as 'causes', even in Davidson's (narrow) conception of causes as anterior events. It is not, then, so much the force of 'because' that need detain us (it has *many* uses, signalling many *diverse* relationships between actions and reasons): rather, it is the unnoticed move in which the term 'has' in 'has a reason' is tacitly being treated in a unitary, 'possessive-ownership' sense. (We saw this gambit operating to the detriment of an argument of John Searle's about the neural locus of 'visual experiences' in the last chapter.) 'Having' signals, contextually, a range of relationships between a subject and grammatical object. Restricting analysis to *one* sense, whereby 'having a reason' is thence misassimilated to states of affairs such as 'having an itch', we are misled. The latter is an *event* which *occurs in* me, and calls forth a response (even if my itch doesn't actually get scratched). The former is *not* an event, nor does it *occur*, and it is nothing which takes place *in(side)* me, neither in my mind nor in my body. My 'having a reason' is my *'being able to tell you* what entitled, justified or excused what I did'.[8]

Of course, there are occasions in which I may actually reflect upon, silently soliloquize (about), why I am about to do what I go on to do. In these circumstances, it may be claimed that I did 'have a reason in mind' prior to acting. Yet such circumstances, even when they are invoked and satisfy the counter-factual conditional – i.e. when it is true that had I *not* explicitly entertained such-and-such a reason I *would not* have performed that action – still cannot qualify as causal on those grounds alone. After all, if I didn't have legs, then I wouldn't have walked to work this morning, I'd have taken a bus, but my having legs didn't *cause* me to walk to work this morning. Moreover, whereas my 'entertaining reason R explicitly prior to acting' *is* an event, it is not identical to 'my having reason R' which, in turn, is *not itself* an event at all, antecedent, coterminous or posterior.

Davidson was aware of facets of the major contrary argument in this field, according to which 'reasons' and 'actions' figure as *logically*, and not contingently, related, and *a fortiori* not causally related. His grasp of this so-called Logical Connection Argument, whose proponents include Winch, Ryle, Melden, Peters and others, is very restricted, however. For Davidson, the only relation which appears to count as a full-blooded 'logical' relationship is that of *entailment*. Thus, he can easily dispose of such a view by remarking that since no particular action entails one specific reason, reason-giving can be informative even if by means of a re-description of the action. Saying 'it's water-soluble and was placed in water' certainly entails, *ceteris paribus*, 'It dissolved', although the converse does not hold.[9] According to Davidson, to say that a man wanted to turn on the light *meant* that he would perform the action which would accomplish this end is to say that his 'primary reason' for flipping the switch entailed that he flipped the switch. However, solubility can be defined in terms of a single test, whereas 'desires cannot be defined in terms of the actions they may rationalise, even though the relation between desire and action is not simply empirical.'[10] Well yes, but why restrict the concept of a 'logical connection' to strict entailments and definitional relations? Elsewhere in his paper,[11] Davidson *contrasts* the 'grammatical' with the 'logical', showing that he is working with a resticted, regimentarian sense of a logical relation, in the sense, perhaps, of Frege or Quine. There is no indication of awareness of the centrality to these arguments of Wittgenstein's concept of 'criterial relation', which is *neither* purely inductive *nor* wholly 'definitional' in the old entailment sense. It is, in this sense, better to speak of a *grammatical* relation between reasons and actions, if the concept of a 'logical' relation is to be consigned exclusively to a propositional calculus from the pre-*Investigations* period.

A 'grammatical' or 'criterial' relation between a (class of) action(s) and a (class of) reason(s) can be given by stating a convention, or a convention plus exemplars and a similarity clause, or by adducing exemplars which illustrate the normative tolerances along with ones which clearly violate such tolerances. It is, for example, not just a poor reason but, taken alone, no reason at all to murder my secretary because of the way she ties her shoelaces. (I say 'taken alone' simply to cancel, for purposes of exposition, the case in which the 'reason' here given is the tip of an enthymematic iceberg – that is, the end of a yet-to-be listed chain or sequence of bridging circumstances which might make the action rational, appropriate or intelligible as so explained. In this instance, were the style of the tying of the shoelaces a give-away as to the hidden identity of the secretary as a spy in my intelligence service, determined on the basis of secret information about an array of possible suspect agents, then my reason may well, under certain circumstances, be not only intelligible but deemed a proper justification). If 'reasons' were contingently and causally, rather than grammatically, linked to actions, then anything might qualify, empirically, as a reason, provided that it (a) antedated the action,

(b) was sincerely avowed and (c) permitted one *no alternative but to* perform the act in question. In some circumstances we may truthfully report (and have our reports ratified as such) that we 'had no choice but to', 'couldn't have done otherwise but to', *X*; we may be said to have been caused to do what we did and in those cases the reasons *were* causally explanatory of the actions. Note, however, that such circumstances are, first, rather exceptional and certainly do not characterize the full range of ordinary human actions with their attendant reasons; and, secondly, that in so far as we are talking about 'causes' here, we are not speaking nomologically (i.e. of lawful regularity or of constant conjunction) but *ethically*. We are claiming *only* that the circumstances absolve us from personal responsibility, that our action is excused, and to the extent that our excuse is accepted, to that extent our causal claim will hold good.

According to Davidson, 'the practical syllogism exhausts its role in displaying an action as falling under one reason; so it cannot be subtilised into a reconstruction of practical reasoning, which involves the weighing of competing reasons.'[12] This may be conceded (for *some* actions) without in any way affecting or undermining the argument which asserts a grammatical, rather than a causal-contingent, relationship between agents' actions and their reasons for them. For, in logical grammar, varieties of reasons may be differentially and contextually-variably related to varieties of actions under diverse normative depictions without this involving either an *infinity* of such relations nor a *singular kind* of relation (e.g. 'rationalization', 'justification', 'conventional entitlement', etc.) between classes of actions and classes of reasons. *Both* the regimented version of the 'logical connection' argument attacked by Davidson and the criterial or 'grammatical' connection argument being defended here concur in the non-randomness of the relationship between reasons and the actions they (can) explain. Where there is a major difference is in the preparedness of proponents of the latter conception to encompass 'normative' latitudes in specifying the boundaries of any logical relations claimed to hold in the domain of reasons and actions. Moreover, since reason-giving is *itself* a kind of action, subject to contextual, normative and conventional constraints, we should not be surprised about this inclusion.

Davidson concludes by arguing that, among those causes which have no agents, are 'those states and changes of state in persons which, because they are reasons as well as causes, make persons voluntary agents'.[13] Here we encounter 'reasons' as 'states and changes of state' which occur or are housed 'in persons' and which, given their causal power, (miraculously) make persons 'voluntary agents'. In what sense could a perfectly common-or-garden reason such as: 'She insulted me', given to explain my action of cursing her, consist in either a 'state' or 'change of state' *inside* me? And why are we to think of such a reason as a cause when I may acknowledge that *I could have done otherwise than* to curse her (thus, I was not compelled, caused, coerced into it by her insulting me) but, curse her I did, and that was my reason?! And how has Davidson so easily circumvented the counter-arguments which posit a contradiction between generically deterministic conceptions of human action and 'voluntariness' as an assignable characteristic of certain of them? Davidson's influential views on causality and human action appear to me to have the support which they do primarily because they buttress, in some way, the possibility of keeping alive a conception of social science as a causal or nomological explanatory enterprise.[14] Alternatively, they are sustained and echoed by those who seek to include human actions within what they take to be a 'causal universe', arguing that to exempt human actions (or most of them) from causality or causal explanation is somehow to indulge in anti-scientific discourse, to render the world mysterious or only theologically accountable. Instead of realizing that what is at stake is a clear analysis of the varied, contextual, grammatically governed workings of our conceptual apparatus in this area, we are led to believe that ontologies are about to crumble, or that suddenly people are theoretically transformed into random units, wholly unpredictable and capable of almost any exercise of unlimited freedom of will. I noted earlier that a commitment to anti-causalism in the domain of (most) human actions (in most circumstances) on logical grounds is not *eo ipso* a commitment to a version of a human world free of constraint, shorn of predictability or limits, a concatenation of purely 'voluntary' agents 'just doing their own thing'.[15]

The Metaphysics of the 'Real Reason'

An aspect of Davidson's views which could profitably be teased out and discussed further concerns the distinction implicit in his thought between the reason(s) for action which may be given, by an agent or by others, which seem to explain his action, and the *real* reason(s) 'underlying' it which 'rouse' or 'move' him to act.[16] Although, as I have said, Davidson tends to conflate 'rationalization' with 'reason' and 'explanation', there is none the less an awareness of the difference between a reason which only seems to explain an action and one which does, indeed, explain it. The latter is reified into a 'state', its 'possession' is objectified into an 'event', and both are projected into agents' heads as causal forces, but leaving all of that to one side, we can still appreciate the distinction and its implications for interactionist, constructionist versions of such phenomena. It would appear that constructionists must perforce blur any distinction between an apparent and a real reason for an action into a matter of practical, discursive negotiation. We have met the 'realist' before in another guise, but here he looms large, threatening to impose his absolutisms upon us yet again. How can he be resisted?

Durkheim assumed that no one could ever really tell from the suicide notes left by the suicided party whether they expressed the 'real' reason for the suicide, and so proposed instead a causal account of suicides which bypassed completely the analysis of such notes and the attendant 'problem of rationalisation'. In his *Rules of Sociological Method*, he had argued:

The sociologist ought, therefore, whether at the moment of the determination of his research objectives or in the course of his demonstrations, to repudiate resolutely the use of concepts originating outside of science for totally unscientific needs. He must emancipate himself from the fallacious ideas that dominate the mind of the layman; he must throw off, once and for all, the yoke of these empirical categories, which, from long continued habit have become tyrannical. At the very least, if at times he is obliged to resort to them, he ought to do so fully conscious of their trifling value, so that he will not assign to them a role out of proportion to their real importance.'[17]

The subsequent treatment of lay reasons for suicide discoverable in, e.g., suicide notes as *in toto coelo* dismissible 'rationalizations' in his famous text, *Suicide*, derived not just from a general skepticism about the possibly self-serving or other-blaming character of such posthumously available communications, but also from a methodological imperative abstracted from Descartes, for whom it served as a philosophical vehicle, and applied to sociological inquiry.

Durkheim's subsequent troubles, conceptual and methodological, which such a 'rule' generated for him, have been amply documented elsewhere.[18] My interest here is to note that, for Durkheim as well as for many subsequent sociological practitioners operating according to similar methodological principles, lay 'reasons for action' have fared badly; they have been standardly treated as 'partial', 'interested', 'distorted', 'ideological', 'truncated', 'mere rationalizations', 'falsely-conscious' and in other ways subjected to theoretical degradation. Such across-the-board rejections of commonsense reasons-for-actions could never work as practical devices of reasoning and judgement in the actual social world shared by sociologist and layperson alike, a world in which one must have some particular, situatedly accountable reason for finding someone's reason to be merely 'rationalizing', 'interest-laden', 'distorted', and the rest. We cannot live by the principle that every lay reason is in some sense defective or non-explanatory, a pot-pourri of 'fallacious ideas ... of trifling value' to use Durkheim's castigatory terms.

At this point, several arguments can develop. One of these simply proposes that, right or wrong, lay reasons must remain irrelevant to sociology's purposes of delivering generalized, causal explanations for conduct. Such a view appears, at best, programmatically self-defeating: if *some* lay reasons are correct explanations of the social conduct they purport to explain, then who needs general causal ones in their stead, and what could be the relationship between the correct lay reasons and the sociologists' causal accounts? I shall not engage with this topic here in its widest ramifications; suffice to note that it forms the basis of much popular dispute in the discipline between 'positivists' of various kinds and anti-positivists, also of various kinds. What I mean to focus upon is the riposte to such an argument which runs as follows: granted, certain lay, commonsense reasons given by agents for the actions in which they engage may well be true, right or correct, *but how are we to tell which ones they are?* If, in the course of our everyday lives, we sometimes make mistakes on this score, get 'taken in' or deceived, misled or cheated, then where could we find the touchstone which could reveal to us, *qua* social scientists, which agents' reasons to believe? How do we ascertain an agent's 'real' reasons for his conduct?

One candidate answer to this question is to assert that an agent's 'real' reason(s) is/are known only to him, and that, in the absence of telepathic channels directly to his mind, we must rest content with guesswork, fallible inference or worse. This reasoning, however, is defective. It *posits* (but cannot really enforce) criteria for the adjudication of a reason's correctness (where 'correctness' is an appropriate dimension of judgement) which are simply not used nor usable in the social world in which such assessments have to be, and are, undertaken and in which the very *concept* of a reason arises and is put to work. The defeasibility of proffered reasons for actions is not an *omnipresent* concern for members of society, and the defeat of a given reason itself requires some reason. Because the tacit or explicit acknowledgement of the correctness of someone's reason may be the upshot of an interactional negotiation, argument or other form of practical engagement involving evidences and pragmatic considerations circumscribed by local arrangements of purposes and projects, we may be inclined, as analysts, to over-generalize from the pragmatic dimensions of such practices to their supposedly essential *contestability*. We may forget that contestation has its occasionality, its times and places, its normative latitudes and 'proper' reasons, and elevate it into a metaphysical or 'transcendental' property of any or all reasons adduced by agents. Wherever we do this, though, we have stripped away all of those features of context and purpose which alone accord to any reason-as-given its actually usable criteria of assessment.

Giving a Reason for an Action is Itself a (Type of) Activity

Our question, how can we tell which of the reasons agents provide do indeed correctly explain their conduct?, which appeared to require of the analyst that he work out some *generic* operational procedure (such as, at best, an algorithm), is, to the extent that it *does* presuppose such a requirement, incapable of being answered. However, if it seeks detailed specifications of the practical logic whereby agents, ourselves included, in their/our various 'walks of life', effect such assessments of each other, then it is a component topic of a research enterprise. That enterprise is concerned to elucidate as fully as possible any logical-methodological property of reasons considered as embedded in, as parts of, courses of situated, practical conduct. As noted earlier, 'giving a reason for an action' is a (kind of) action itself, and fully amenable to analysis for its variable manifestations and their logic of production *in situ*, from the ordinary, casual conversation to the drama of a courtroom determination. Reason-avowals and attributions (whether these be in the form of purposes, intentions, motives, conventions, desires or kindred accounts, and whether they are designed to excuse, justify or entitle the actions they seek to explain) are empirical social phenomena.

Among the first sociologists systematically to treat 'reasons for action' as sociological phenomena were Scott and Lyman in two well-known articles on 'accounts'.[19] Their concern was to highlight the *conventionality* of accounts, especially excuses and justifications for particular classes of activities. In some respects, their analysis was an extension of one of its chief sources of inspiration, the work of Mills on 'vocabularies of motive'.[20] However, Scott and Lyman gloss over many aspects of the logic of reason-giving, tending to restrict themselves to two classes of reasons, excuses and justifications (omitting any reference to entitlement-claims, for example), which are occasioned by perceived deviations of various kinds from expected or normatively enjoined conduct. This leads them to over-generalize one possible function into a stable property, as when they assert that such accounts 'prevent conflict from arising by verbally bridging the gap between action and expectation'.[21] But don't '*poor* excuses' and '*insufficient* justifications' characteristically occasion interactional problems, even conflicts? And aren't many 'accounts' which constitute reasons for action *or* inaction components of combative, assertive or rejecting communications?

We shall see further on that a more *detailed* approach to the analysis of these phenomena is required.

Scott and Lyman distinguish between four 'modalities' of excuse-formulation (appeals to accidents, appeals to defeasibility, appeals to biological drives and scapegoating), and six techniques of justification (denial of injury, denial of victim, condemnation of the condemner(s), appeal to loyalties, the 'sad tale' and 'self-fulfilment'). They further specify and illustrate five sociolinguistic styles of account delivery: the intimate, casual, consultative, formal and 'frozen'. One of their most suggestive proposals, however, is that '*every account is a manifestation of the underlying negotiation of identities'*[22] of the parties. This insight has since been elaborated by Jayyusi in her extensive analysis of the logic of person-categorization and its relationship to action-ascription and account-production (the design of reasons for actions)[23]. Among the many ways in which membership categories (or social identities) can work in communicative interaction is to furnish 'grounds' for acting in particular ways in particular circumstances; often, a single such category invocation will suffice in this respect, as when someone replies to a query such as: 'Why are you doing that?' with a categorial self-identification such as: 'I'm a police officer', or 'Why did he do that?' with 'He's just a vandal'. However, as Jayyusi remarks: 'it seems as though the distinction between doing an activity for no specific reason outside that activity and doing it for a reason (purpose, motive, interest) beyond the activity itself is one that is important for members in their categorisation of persons.[24]

Endotychistic[25] actions, actions which are intelligibly seen or claimed as undertaken for their own sake, can be consequential for the categorization of their producers, as when we find that a teenage 'hustler' has engaged in a homosexual act without demanding payment, thus becoming eligible for re-categorization as a 'queer',[26] or when a person is found to have stolen for the sake of stealing and is no longer a 'thief' but a 'kleptomaniac', or when someone is found to have injured someone for the sake of injuring him and is characterizable as a 'sadist' or 'psychopath', etc.[27] It is important here to keep in mind that some categories where ascribed to persons can furnish generic 'reasons' for actions or manner of acting when interactants literally determine *no* (good enough, sufficient, convincing, etc.) reason whatever, as in the case of 'He(she) is mentally ill'[28].

In explicating 'reason-giving' as comprising an array of situated activity types, conversation analysts have revealed a variety of interesting properties. When 'reasons' are treated as empirical 'conversational' (or, more broadly, as 'communicative') phe-nomena, it becomes clear from an inspection of transcriptions of naturally produced social interactions that their *sequential position* is variously consequential for their design and reception. Atkinson and Drew, in their well-known study of court trials,[29] note that sociologists' use of the concept of 'account' in the study of the social management of 'deviance'[30] encourages analysts 'to look for *the* account which a possible offender gives for his action, as though there was just one such object – where the close examination of most court cases . . . reveals that there is no single component which carries all the work which a witness or defendant does to defend his action.'[31] Where 'reasons for action' *are* relatively discrete communicative phenomena, such as in those instances where they comprise a single utterance or turn-at-talk, their placement is very often adjacent to an accusation, blaming or complaint rather than simply following a question/request for information. Such placement is consequential for how 'reasons' are designed and proposedly to-be-received by recipients.

Evidence is beginning to show that, in sequential environments where a blame ascription has been made (e.g., through a complaint) or is anticipated, recipients design their turns so as to avoid self-blame. Speakers may exhibit the dispreferred character of actions which accept self-blame partly through their overwhelming use of the turn-types which disavow blame-ascriptions (i.e., denials, justifications, etc.), but also through their design of turns in which the dispreferred types occur. For example, apologies – which appear to accept self-blame – are very often given with accounts or 'defence' components, so that turns containing apologies are generally organised as [Apologies] + [Defences].[32]

Referring to the distinction between 'Justifications' and 'Excuses' as types of reasons-for-actions, Atkinson and Drew observe that such communicative objects can be found to have a differential sequential ordering:

the former (justificatory) objects occurring in a prior position in blame sequences, the latter (excuse-type) objects being done in a subsequent position, as a 'second-best' strategy. Hence, instead of seeking analytically constitutive features of these 'speech acts', they can be identified as, conventionally (i.e., for speakers), preferred and less preferred defence strategies.'[33]

However, it should be kept in mind that, whilst speech-acts such as Justifications and Excuses are not uniformly and unproblematically so identifiable in discourse, none the less they do belong to "members"' vernacular ways of depicting each others' activities, so that one way of enacting a 'preferred defence strategy' is, exactly, to produce a well-fitted, hearable Justification. In this sense, they do not necessarily function as mutually exclusive alternative characterizations.

In a recent, unpublished dissertation, Beattie has extended the empirical domain for the analysis of 'reason-giving' from courtroom settings to other arenas of interaction.[34] Still concentrating upon blaming sequences as environments within which reasons-for-action are conventionally produced activities, she focuses upon reason-giving practices within 'standing relationships' (especially 'husband–wife' pairs), and documents a wide variety of contextually transformable orientations to facets of those relationships which not only place implicit constraints upon, but which are *embodied* or *displayed* in, conventionalized forms of reason-giving. Since any action can be explained in a variety of different ways, any *actually* produced way of explaining it can be found to exhibit features of locally transformable, negotiable kinds. Lynch's study of pre-trial arguments[35] also shows how the actual sequential production of reason-giving can display the changing orientations of its producer(s) to a sense of locally developing relevancies without witnessably undermining the 'integrity', 'implicit truth-claim' or 'sincerity' of the reason(s) preferred.

'Reason-giving', in all of its forms, is organized by tacit orientations to such sociological phenomena as: the situatedly assignable membership categories of its producers and recipients, the sequential placement of the activity within a course of communicative interaction, a shared *or* divergent but *displayed* sense of the nature and purpose of the occasion/setting of co-participation, the emergence of topical relevances between parties to an interaction, the negotiable characterisation of the act or actions[36] for which one or more reasons are sought and/or delivered, and kindred (explicable) considerations. In conducting our inquiries into such phenomena, we do not need unilaterally to stipulate *competing* reasons-for-actions as sociologists. This is not because we must uncritically accept anything a member offers as his reason for doing what he did/does, but because reason-giving itself is an investigable mode of human activity, as complex and as intriguing as any other achievement of practical action. As socially constructed, communicative phenomena, they have barely begun to be explored.

Notes

1   As reprinted in his Alan R. White (ed.), *The Philosophy of Action* (Oxford University Press, Oxford, 1977 edn)

2   Ibid., p. 80.

3   Ibid., p. 81.

4   Ibid.

5   Ibid., p. 85.

6   Ibid, emphasis in original.

7   Ibid., p. 87.

8   A.R. Louch is still our best guide through these thickets. See his 'Reasons'. In *Explanation and Human Action* (Basil Blackwell, Oxford, 1966). The propensity to treat ability and capacity concepts as if they were state or event concepts is nicely elaborated and criticized in G.P. Baker and P.M.S. Hacker, *Wittgenstein on Meaning and Understanding*, pp. 597–602. Additionally, one wonders how Davidson would square a case of my acting in an admittedly bad, undesirable fashion and then adducing an excuse for my action as the reason that explains it with his insistence upon the omni-relevance of a 'pro attitude' in 'primary reasons' for action?

9   Davidson's example, 'Actions, Reasons and Causes', p. 90.

10   Ibid.

11   Ibid., p. 89.

12   Ibid., p. 91.

13   Ibid., p. 94.

14   For an example of this, see R. Keat and John Urry, *Social Theory as Science* (Routledge & Kegan Paul, London, 1975). For a treatment in which Davidsonian arguments are accepted in the context of a commitment to quite *different* goals for social science, see G. Macdonald and P. Pettit, *Semantics and Social Science* (Routledge & Kegan Paul, London, 1981).

15   Various quite outrageous parodies of ethnomethodological inquiry appear to promulgate such a view. See, for example, Ernest Gellner's notorious article, 'Ethnomethodology' The Re-Enchantment Industry or the California Way of Subjectivity', *Philosophy of the Social Sciences*, Vol. 5, 1975. But then Gellner never understood Winch or Wittgenstein either. See Michael Dummett's 'Ordinary Language'. In his *Truth and Other Enigmas* (Duckworth, London, 1978) for an impartial critique of Gellner's recurrent misconceptions on this score.

16   Davidson himself deploys 'determine' ('Actions, Reasons and Causes', p. 91) to specify the relation of 'reasons' to 'choice, decision and behavior'. Alasdair MacIntyre, in the course of proposing similar views in his 'The Idea of a Social Science', in Bryan R. Wilson (ed.),

Rationality (Basil Blackwell, Oxford, 1974), uses the expressions 'productive of action', 'moved to action' and 'roused to action' in connection with reasons (pp. 116–17).

17 Emile Durkheim, *The Rules of Sociological Method*, ed. G.E.G. Catlin (Free Press, N.Y., 1964), p. 32.

18 *Inter alia*, by Harvey Sacks, 'On Sociological Description', *Berkeley Journal of Sociology*, Vol. 8, 1963 and J.M. Atkinson, *Discovering Suicide* (Macmillan, London, 1978).

19 Marvin B. Scott and Stanford M. Lyman, 'Accounts', *American Sociological Review*, Vol. 33, December 1968, reprinted in J.G. Manis and B.N. Meltzer (eds), *Symbolic Interaction* (Allyn & Bacon, Boston, 1972, 2nd edn), and their 'Accounts, Deviance and Social Order'. In Jack D. Douglas (ed.), *Deviance and Respectability: The Social Construction of Moral Meanings* (Basic Books, N.Y., 1970). See also Laurie Taylor, 'The Significance and Interpretation of Replies to Motivational Questions: The Case of Sex Offenders', *Sociology*, Vol. 9, January 1975.

20 C. Wright Mills, 'Situated Actions and Vocabularies of Motive'. In Manis and Meltzer, (eds), *Symbolic Interaction*.

21 Scott and Lyman, in ibid., p. 405.

22 Ibid., p. 424, emphasis in original.

23 Lena Jayyusi, *Categorization and the Moral Order* (Routledge & Kegan Paul, London, 1984).

24 Ibid., p. 187.

25 D. S. Shwayder, *The Stratification of Behavior* (Routledge & Kegan Paul, London, 1965), p. 160, develops an analysis of such activity types.

26 See Albert Reiss's perceptive study, 'The Social Integration of Queers and Peers'. In Howard S. Becker (ed.), *The Other Side* (Free Press, Glencoe, 1964).

27 See Jayyusi, *Categorization*, p. 187.

28 For an analysis of 'mental illness' as a component of action-account schemata, see Dorothy Smith, ' "K" Is Mentally Ill: The Anatomy of a Factual Account', *Sociology*, Vol. 12, No. 2, 1978.

29 J.M. Atkinson and Paul Drew, *Order in Court: The Organisation of Verbal Interaction in Judicial Settings* (Macmillan, London, 1979).

30 E.g. by Scott and Lyman. In Manis and Meltzer, *Symbolic Interaction*; and by R.M. Emerson, *Judging Delinquents* (Aldine, Chicago, 1969), *passim*.

31 Atkinson and Drew, *Order in Court*, pp. 139–40.

32 Ibid., p. 60.

33 Ibid., p. 141.

34 Martha C. Beattie, 'Practices of Blaming and Explaining: An

Ethnomethodological Approach'. Unpublished PhD dissertation, Department of Sociology, Boston University, 1987.

35   Michael Lynch, 'Closure and Disclosure in Pre-Trial Argument', *Human Studies*, Vol. 5, No. 4, 1982.

36   For a succinct discussion of the linguistic devices whereby an action's identification may be differentially individuated, see Joel Feinberg's 'Action and Responsibility'. In Alan R. White (ed.), *The Philosophy of Action*. In particular, Feinberg, drawing upon J.L. Austin's path-breaking insights in his 'A Plea for Excuses' (*Philosophical Papers*, Oxford University Press, Oxford, 1961), developed the concept of an 'accordion effect' in the description/ascription of actions: 'because an act, like the folding musical instrument, can be squeezed down to a minimum or else stretched out. He turned the key, he opened the door, he startled Smith, he killed Smith – all of these are things we might say that Jones *did* with one identical set of bodily movements . . . . We can, if we wish, puff out an action to include an effect, and more often than not our language obliges us by providing a relatively complex action word for the purpose. Instead of saying Smith did *A* (a relatively simple act) and thereby caused *X* in *Y*, we might say something of the form 'Smith *X*-ed *Y*'; instead of "Smith opened the door causing Jones to be startled", "Smith startled Jones"' (Feinberg, in White (ed.), pp. 106–7). Several points emerge of relevance to our interests here. First, before any 'reason' can be intelligibly (grammatically, in the broad Wittgensteinian sense) related to an action, the action must, as Davidson noted, be 'under a (particular) description': Feinberg's point shows that a transformation of the description of an action thereby transforms the domain of possibilities for adducing a reason for it. Secondly, some characterizations of actions can display, 'built-in', so to speak, a reason which informed its production. Thus, to say of someone that he 'committed euthanasia' is *at least* to say of him that he killed someone with the purpose of putting him out of his misery. That *other*, independent reasons may *also* be furnished does not affect this point. Thirdly, a successful transformation of an action-ascription from, say, 'he killed *X*' to 'he murdered *X*' can be instructive as to the *intentionality* of the act. However, although it may be true to say of John that he 'entertained his friends', if such entertainment was achieved by murdering someone, the elision of act with consequence is subject to a charge of under-attribution. On this and related matters pertaining to the ascription of action, see Eric D'Arcy, *Human Acts: An Essay in Their Moral Evaluation* (Clarendon Press, Oxford, 1963). For an original socio-logical elaboration of this issue, see Jayyusi, *Categorization*, chapter 6.

Concluding Remarks

Much of what I have argued in these pages is at variance with established theoretical and meta-theoretical positions in those intellectual disciplines currently concerned with 'cognitive' studies, although there is a growing interest in the possibilities and prospects afforded by such reconsiderations.

I have documented several aspects of a shift of interest in contemporary sociology of knowledge away from restricting its scope to the exploration of purely historical, macro-level connections between political doctrines and ideologies/utopias and the general social circumstances of their origin and distribution. The transition to a broader interest in the functioning of all varieties of 'commonsense' knowledge (both propositional or discursive knowledge and practical, non-discursive 'knowing-how'), as well as differentiated forms of specialist (particularly 'scientific') knowledge in a society, was seen to re-establish, on a rigorous basis, a relationship between the interests of the sociology of action, interaction and communication on the one hand and those of a properly 'epistemic' sociology on the other. Such a recasting of this relationship involves a methodological shift away from the construction of causal-explanatory models for epistemic social phenomena and toward a project of articulating the manifold 'logical', conceptual and grammatical features of such phenomena as they are empirically available. In essence, the problematics of 'intelligibility' as a feature of any recurrent sociocultural phenomenon becomes the central topic. Thus, for example, instead of asking 'What causes members M to believe X or Y (rather than Z)?', the inquiry focuses upon such questions as 'On what basis is epistemic property *X* or *Y* assignable to any *P* by members of society or collectivity *S*?', 'What relationships obtain between activity *A* and reasoning *R* or belief *B*?', 'How is the manifest intelligibility of social phenomenon *P* achievable by members *M*?' or 'What is the grammar of the deployment of the concept or category *C* by *M* in circumstances *S*?' A substantial contribution to the reformulation of the contemporary sociology of knowledge along such 'epistemic' lines has been made by work in ethnomethodology, conceptual analysis in the Wittgensteinian and Austinian traditions and the broadly 'social constructionist' approach of Schutzian social phenomenology.

Within the program and perspective of such an 'epistemic', socio-logical enterprise, it is argued that a fundamental reassessment of a variety of traditional problems is made possible, especially those of 'imputation' and 'relativism'. Further, increasing clarity about the differential roles of *knowledge*-ascription and avowal and *belief*-ascription and avowal as specific social practices is facilitated. The role of attributions of knowledge/belief in the domain of perceptual claims, both historical and contemporaneous, for example, becomes investigable. However, the most basic transformation of perspective suggested by developments in this new field concerns the theoretical characterization of the nature of the so-called 'cognitive' and/or 'mental' endowments of persons.

It has long been a conventional wisdom in the sociology of interaction that agents do not merely react or respond to stimuli: human action is not reducible to human *re*action, and human interaction is not reducible nor generally identical to human inter-*stimulation*. Rather, human agents orient to the 'meaning(s)' which utterances, non-linguistic actions, objects, places, circumstances, etc. are seen to 'have' for them. Agents are depicted as endlessly involved in 'interpreting' the 'meaning(s)' of their environing phenomena of relevance. 'Understanding' and 'interpreting' are construed as identical, and treated theoretically as interior mental processes of registering 'meanings'. Observers, lay and professional, can only grasp these 'understandings/ interpretations' through inference or analogy, and the closer they can make themselves resemble the subjects in question (e.g. by 'participant-observational involvements' with them), the more reliable become their inferences. Many of these conceptions involve fundamental conceptual errors. Understanding and interpreting are different (and diverse) phenomena. The former is akin to an ability or, in some circumstances, an achievement, and is never properly analysed as a process; the latter is a quite specifically restricted undertaking. Moreover, people have mundane ways of exhibiting their understandings (as well as their misunderstandings) to which we are blinded by mentalistic misconceptions according to which 'understanding' takes place exclusively 'in the mind'. Although inferential work is sometimes required (and, where required, is itself rule-governed or conventionally constrained), discerning that, and what, someone understands is not generically an *inferential* accomplishment. A corollary to this is to note that 'meaning-as-intelligibility' and 'meaning-as-personal-significance' must be distinguished. Basic forms of comprehension pertain primarily to the former. Although the primary interest of epistemic sociology becomes the analysis of the achievement of social intelligibility rather than the documentation of the vagaries of idiosyncratically personal significances which phenomena may be thought to have, it is worth noting that the discernment of the latter is not achieved by members exclusively through precariously inferential moves: the personal significance of a phenomenon for someone can be variously – and non-inferentially – *displayed* in their witnessable linguistic and other forms of conduct in various circumstances. And inferring a 'personal significance' for someone from situationally 'inconclusive evidences' is itself a mundane social practice governed by investigable conventions of reasoning in diverse settings.

We have spoken of intelligibility (of utterances, activities, interactions, events, objects, places, personal attributes, etc.) as 'grammatically' circumscribed. Alternative formulations of this point include such characterizations as 'rule-governed', 'conventionally constrained' and 'criterially bounded'. No general uniformity exists among the types of rules, conventions and criteria which are found socially to control the possibilities or options for making sense of phenomena, and no rule taken 'in itself', so to speak, prescribes in advance of its application everything that may be relevant to an assessment of compliance to it. Such considerations cannot be used in arguments for 'rule-skepticism', however, unless the proponent is assuming a stipulatively restricted concept of a rule, convention or criterion. Even when the phenomena in question are those of 'inner experience' (pains, dreams), it is a grammatically circumscribed conceptual apparatus, which is *intersubjectively* acquired and deployed 'in the first instance' (and in most subsequent 'instances' of their use), which renders all such phenomena intelligible, even to their experiencers as matters of first-person avowability. Various elements of the classical argument from Wittgenstein were given to support the view that there cannot be a purely 'private language' of the mental or experiential domains, and some recent counter-arguments were considered and rejected.

The notion that intelligibility is intersubjective and grammatically circumscribed should not be confused with the idea, currently popular in cognitive science theorizing, that human agents are engaged in continuous sequences of 'unconscious mental processing' of 'informational inputs' from an 'environment'. Several incoherences and misleading disanalogies in such a 'computationalist' conception were exposed, and its essentially neo-Cartesian roots revealed.

The illusionary thesis that our 'minds' are populated with 'mental entities' of which we attain knowledge by mysterious interior analogues to our corporeal senses animates a good deal of psychologistic theorizing in the human sciences, and can only be unravelled by piecemeal conceptual considerations. In particular, false equivalences between commonalities of form and commonalities of sense need to be exposed, and a propensity to treat (first-person) avowals of various mental predicates either as species of 'object descriptions', as 'corrigible theoretical assertions' or as 'subjectively sovereign claims', requires correction. Other mystifying reifications in the domains of 'personality characteristics', 'special subjective states', and their properties, are ripe for refutation. All of these arguments pave the way for an uncluttered incorporation of the phenomena of mind, experience and cognition into an epistemic sociology.

A pervasive theoretical standpoint in the human sciences, although articulated with diverse emphases, favors the view that human actions are amenable to one or another form of causal-explanatory accounting couched in the theoretical terms of the inquiring discipline: thus, for a good deal of sociology and social psychology, conduct is to be explained by reference to generalizable causal factors operating in the social environment(s) or social structures within which persons live their lives; for much neuropsychology and cognitive-science theorizing, conduct is treated as causally explainable with reference to neural or neural-computational 'mechanisms' of theoretically describable sorts, and for some psychological approaches, conduct is to be causally explained with reference to measurable arrays of physical stimuli originating in the material environment or with reference to features of 'personality' type. All such theoretical commitments assume a certain stance on the issue of the relationship of 'reasons for action' and 'causes of action', one in which agents' 'reasons' are dis-privileged and rendered epiphenomenal as 'explanation' candidates. The controversy in the philosophy of the social sciences surrounding this issue has raged for some years, and many participants in the debate have been persuaded of the viability of the 'Davidsonian solution', in which no incompatibility is seen between 'reason-explanation' and 'causal explanation' in the sphere of human actions *qua* actions: 'having a reason' is itself one kind of 'causal' factor operative in human conduct. I have tried to show here that such reasoning embodies a number of fallacious moves, and to reinstate reason-explanations *not* as competitors with any particular theoretical explanations of human actions (there cannot logically be any such competition) but as phenomena of communicative praxis in their own right.

However, such a move is compatible with, indeed (I think) requires, a fundamental reconsideration of the goal of analysis of human conduct and cognition. If theoretical reifications of the mental and of the personality cannot serve as genuine explanatory 'mechanisms', then many psychologistic explanation-strategies fail. If human conduct is emergent from and not identical to the bodily functioning which enters into it, then various forms of neurophysiological and computationalist determinisms do not even approach the phenomena of interest here. If sociological and social-psychological 'explanatory variables' extracted by researchers from unilateral descriptions of 'social environments' or 'social structures' simply omit members' practical judgemental and orientational relevances, then they must deliver theoretical claims of unknown relationship to these relevances. Whatever schema one selects, the problematics of reason-giving praxis is neglected to its detriment. Attempts to elevate members' actually given reasons themselves to the level of theoretically pertinent explanations do not settle the question, either: there are no principled procedures for establishing generically either the validity or the invalidity of proffered reasons, and no point in abstracting 'essences' from their contextualized variety. In place of seeking general 'explanations of human conduct', then, an epistemic sociology must insist upon the propriety of the goal of 'explications' of their socio-logical properties, their *possibilities* of production and their *grammatical* connections to other components of the conceptual apparatus (e.g. situatedly relevant conceptualizations of agent, location, experience, personality, mind, context, and so forth).

Some of the issues articulated in this (brief) overview have been more fully explored elsewhere: all that I have sought to achieve in these pages has been to present a sketch, where helpful, of the intellectual origins of the major topics and concepts, chart some of the more prominent contributions, illustrate some of the more interesting themes with examples and suggest some directions for further elaboration. In particular, I have selected for logical (and sometimes critical) scrutiny some of what I take to be the more interesting alternative standpoints available in the field.

One especially contentious claim advanced in this text is the proposal for a 'grammatical' interest in epistemic or cognitive phenomena without endorsing the traditional dichotomy usually connected to such an interest – that of the 'conceptual' and the 'empirical' – whereby the analyst is quite unnecessarily restricted to requiring *exclusively* 'invented' instances or examples as 'data' when working out the practical logic of the conceptual, epistemic domains of interest to him.

The central focus of the present treatment, however, has been the problematics of the human agent considered as a 'cognitive' being, endowed with a 'mind' and a 'personality', who navigates through a social world employing such 'subjective' equipment in diverse ways. What I have tried to show, in various ways and through different kinds of examples and arguments, are the limitations and pecularities of thinking this way about the relationships between a person and his sociocultural environments and circumstances. I have tried to show that theoretical schemes which place the individual human agent at center-stage and build uncritically upon assumptions of an atomistic, psychologistic and cognitivist kind, fail to do justice either to the nature of the personal and 'mental' attributes of people or to the ways in which these actually connect with the culture and society which they significantly *instantiate* as well as co-produce in living their lives.

Entrenched paradigms of thought are hard to shift. One chief reason for directing this work primarily at students is the hope that they will not be so wedded to the orthodox precepts of their disciplines that they will be in a better position to fulfil the function Kuhn assigned, in a strangely (for him) unsociological way, to 'conversion' between scientific protagonists of diverse paradigmatic commitments or to the physical demise of such paradigm-bearers – the transformation of the paradigms themselves. If this work, in company with others of its kind, fails to stimulate such a development, at least it may have provided some of the ammunition required for raising the tricky questions . . .

Index